THE FILMS OF STEPHEN KING

MORE WILDSIDE CLASSICS

THE FILMS OF STEPHEN KING

by

MICHAEL R. COLLINGS

WILDSIDE PRESS

To Ralph & Thella Collings
and
Jack & Dorothy Reeve:

who have freely given more love and support than
anyone could ask for or expect.

THE FILMS OF STEPHEN KING

This edition published in 2006 by Wildside Press, LLC.
www.wildsidepress.com

Table of Contents

FOREWORD

The Films of Stephen King, the fifth in the Starmont series of critical studies, comes to its readers under false colors.

It is <u>not</u> about the films of Stephen King--or only partially so, since some chapters will discuss films that are King's: <u>Creepshow</u>, with King participating as screenwriter and actor; <u>Cat's Eye</u> and <u>Silver Bullet</u>, with King again as screenwriter; and <u>Overdrive</u>, with him as screenwriter and director.

These are <u>Stephen King's</u> films.

And then there are the others: <u>Children of the Corn</u>, for instance, which deviated so radically from King's original conception that he received no screenplay credits at all. Or <u>The Shining</u>, which has already been called "Kubrick's Shining" to distinguish Stanley Kubrick's cinematic vision from King's novel.

The listing could go on, of course, but we would simply be re-working the table of contents.

The simple fact is that King's stories and novels have provided a wealth of material for filmmakers. Almost every novel published under King's name (and two of the Bachman novels) has been produced as a film, is in production, or has been optioned. Some, like <u>Carrie</u>, followed immediately upon the appearance of the novel; in the case of <u>Carrie</u>, in fact, the movie helped make King better known. Others, specifically <u>The Stand</u>, have been in production for years, caught in the complications of reducing King's expansive prose to a two-, three-, or four-hour visual format. Still others, such as <u>The Talisman</u>, have barely gone beyond the stage of optioning. In a rare case such as <u>Silver Bullet</u>, an expansion of <u>Cycle of the Werewolf</u>, the film actually allowed King to revise his original prose version.

Nor have producers stopped at King's novels. Some years ago King commented that every story but one in <u>Night Shift</u> had been discussed as a film project; with the publication of <u>Skeleton Crew</u> last year, producers have an even richer source of

1

materials. <u>The Twilight Zone</u> broadcast "Gramma" on Valentine´s Day, 1986; <u>Tales from the Darkside</u> included "Word Processor of the Gods" during its 1984 season. And other stories seem naturals for film: "The Raft," "The Monkey," "The Mist," "The Reach."

The interest in King´s fiction transcends professional levels as well. In addition to attracting such eminent names as Brian de Palma, Stanley Kubrick, David Cronenberg, John Carpenter, George A. Romero, and Steven Spielberg, King´s fictions have drawn the attention of neophytes. One such production, Frank Darabont´s <u>The Woman in the Room</u> is among the finest translations of King from print to screen. The advertisement in <u>Variety</u> announcing the film´s debut on Los Angeles public television (September 17, 1985) carried King´s comment that

> THE WOMAN IN THE ROOM is clearly the best of the short films made from my stuff. The direction, acting, and cinematography are all excellent. I´d have to say I was deeply affected . . . due in large part to [Darabont´s] ability as a filmmaker.

The kudo was well deserved. It doesn´t require big budgets or big-name stars to do justice to King´s fictions; on the other hand, it requires more than budget or stars or a King title to make a film communicate King´s unique touch.

What this book is interested in, then, is not just the films of Stephen King, but films by and from King, films based (however loosely) on King´s fiction, films that attempt to translate the texture of his prose into another medium.

Like any form of translation, such attempts seem almost doomed from the beginning. In translating a poem from one language to another, for example, the translator may remain true to the form and structure of the original, and by doing so produce something that is neither poetically nor idiomatically consistent with the second language. Or the translator can ignore the rigidity of form and structure and translate the essence of the original. In this case, the result may be a poem, but it will probably have little in common with the original; it may even reflect the translator's skills more than the poet's.

In King's case, the translations are particularly difficult. With the exception of Carrie, Cycle, and the short stories, his works are long; the major difficulty in preparing The Stand for the screen, for example, is cutting down an 800-plus page novel to a three- or four-hour format. By the time the screenplay has approached a usable length, the narrative has lost much of its resemblance to King's novel. At the other extreme, the thirty or so pages of "Children of the Corn" had to be padded unmercifully to create a full-length film. In neither case is the finished product essentially the same as King's prose original.

Compounding all of this is the additional fact that directors, producers, cinematographers, and actors all bring their individual visions to a project. King has said frequently that once a property is purchased for film, he worries little about it. The book still exists, solid and stable on a library shelf; nothing can alter the text itself, no matter how divergent the film may be.

King's comment tacitly accepts the most critical point in dealing with novel-into-film. The visual arts differ in essence from the verbal; their techniques, purposes, and successes grow out of different possibilities. In one sense, to compare a novel to its film version seems an exercise in futility. If it is translated directly, there seems little purpose in having the film at all. If it is translated more loosely, to the point that the director or producer or screenwriter alters the substance of the narrative itself, the result is an entirely different and often unrelated creation. To take a classic example--the changes Howard Hawks and Christian Nyby introduced into their 1951 film The Thing (From Another World), based on John W. Campbell's "Who Goes There?," shift the directions of nearly every imagistic, thematic, or symbolic pattern in the original story. The result is a fine film, but one no longer recognizably derived from Campbell's text. Carpenter's restoration of Campbell's setting, characters' names, and protean creature from space seems truer to the original, but its emphasis on gory special effects angles it into yet another direction. Instead of a single arti-

3

fact, readers and viewers may choose from three: Campbell's verbal performance, the original visual re-creation by Hawks and Nyby, or Carpenter's subsequent film.

To complicate matters even further, Alan Dean Foster carried the translation process a step further, writing a novel based on a screenplay by Bill Lancaster (according to the dust jacket of Bantam's book club edition) and on Campbell's short story (according to the title page). By doing so, he again alters the narrative, developing Carpenter's implicit visual symbolism more fully; the conclusion of the film implies a stalemate, for example, while Foster uses a literal game of chess to emphasize the ambiguous ending of his novel. Childs and Macready, the white and black kings as it were, square off again; and amid the dying flames that destroyed (?) the Thing, "Macready nudged a pawn two squares forward . . . " (181).

While the history of the multiple manifestations of "The Thing" may seem to have little relevance to Stephen King and film, it does illustrate more completely than most narratives the intricate relationship between word and image, between verbal performance and visual. With King's works, the process rarely reaches such intricate states; at this point, we have only a single prose text and a single film to work with for most. But the permutations introduced by Hawks and Nyby into Campbell's prose, by Carpenter into Campbell's story and into the 1951 film, and by Foster into all three characterize what happened to King's works during their transformations into films. The Films of Stephen King concerns the inevitable seesaw between author and filmmaker, with narrative as the fulcrum separating them. Fortunately, most of the films in question are readily available on videocassette, allowing for something approximating the close critical examination of a printed text.

As before, many people have helped to make this book a reality: my family, with their patience while I immured myself in the back room with the word processor; Barbara Bolan and Sandy Parigan through their diligence as collectors; Al and Bill Reveles of Video Pavilion (Westlake

Village CA) for their help in finding the films on videocassette; Lee Finley for locating several primary sources; and Dan Klamkin and Ted Dikty for their unflagging enthusiasm for collecting and criticism.

In addition, I must extend my gratitude to Dean John Wilson, Dr. James Smythe of the Humanities Division, and the Reassigned Time Committee of Seaver College for allowing me released time in the fall of 1985 to work on this project.

And, of course, deepest thanks to Stephen King.

Michael R. Collings
Thousand Oaks, California
May 1986

ABBREVIATIONS

Art	Stephen King: The Art of Darkness, by Douglas E. Winter (NAL, 1984)
CR	Castle Rock: The Stephen King Newsletter
Cycle	Cycle of the Werewolf (1981)
DM	Danse Macabre (1981)
DS	Different Seasons (1982)
DSK	Discovering Stephen King, ed. Darrell Schweitzer (Starmont 1985)
DZ	The Dead Zone (1979)
FI	Fear Itself, ed. Tim Underwood and Chuck Miller (Underwood-Miller, 1982; NAL, 1984)
LW	The Long Walk ("Bachman," 1979)
MF	The Many Facets of Stephen King, by Michael R. Collings (Starmont, 1985
NS	Night Shift (1978)
PS	Pet Sematary (1983)
RG/SK	Reader´s Guide to Stephen King, by Douglas E. Winter (Starmont, 1982)
RM	The Running Man ("Bachman," 1982)
RW	Roadwork ("Bachman," 1981)
SC	Skeleton Crew (1985)
SK/RB	Stephen King as Richard Bachman by Michael R. Collings (Starmont, 1985)
SL	´Salem´s Lot (1975)
SW	The Shorter Works of Stephen King, by Michael R. Collings and David A. Engebretson (Starmont, 1985)

CHAPTER I

Novel Versus Film

In speaking of "The Death and Rebirth of the Novel," Leslie A. Fiedler makes several important points about the form and function of the novel as literature. It is, he contends, an essentially popularist form, derived, not from "traditional High Literary Art (an art dependent on limited literacy)" or from "Folk Literary Art (an art dependent on mass illiteracy)," but rather related more directly to that which followed it: "the comic strip, the comic book, cinema, TV" (189). As the novel entered the technological age, innovations in production and distribution emphasized the popular elements of the form, expanding it to the level of a "mass art within the limits of literacy." And even more critically, according to Fiedler, it grew closer and closer to the visual media which, by replacing word with image, "furthered the disjunction between being able to apprehend a tale and acquiring the ´standards´ associated exclusively with books for judging its ´value´" (190).

While reaction to Stephen King´s fictions from readers at the popular level as well as from "establishment" critics would support Fiedler´s assertions in this particular, he proceeds to make an even more important statement in defining the implicit relation between novel and film. After speaking of the historical tendency of readers (and other authors) to treat characters from novels as belonging to a form of Public Domain--for example, when an author appropriates a Dickens character and writes a new series of adventures about it, a process recently repeated with <u>Star Trek</u> and <u>Star Wars</u> characters--Fiedler notes that

There is finally, and quite regardless of the will of the original author, a special affinity between the authentic (i.e., mythic) novel and the cinema; so

9

that it sometimes seems as if all such
novels want to metamorphose into movies,
being merely the embryos of the films
they finally become, a kind of chrysalis
yearning to be a butterfly. And there
is a rude justice in this development,
since, from the start, certain popular
novelists apparently yearned for,
dreamed the invention of, the movies--
Sir Walter Scott, for instance, creating
effects (he loved to be called "the master of motion") which in their rapidity
and scope need the movie camera and the
broad screen to fulfill them. (190)

While Fiedler does not refer specifically to King,
his comments reflect one of the common perceptions
about King's fiction and about his style--that
both are tied into the visual imagination.

Paul Gray's review of Different Seasons refers to King as the "Master of Postliterate
Prose," a phrase King dislikes (and with good reason). In spite of that dislike, however, Gray is
correct on one point: King's fictions do appeal to
the visual imagination; by means of the metaphors,
similes, comparisons, and images which thread
through them, they invite the readers to see the
action of the narrative through cinematic images.

In The Talisman, to take a recent example,
King and Straub speak of Osmond's smell as reminiscent of "those old black-and-white British
films where some poor guy was on trial in the Old
Bailey" (98); Jack's experiences in the Mill Road
tunnel remind him of the Roadrunner cartoons
(124); the police car in Oatley looks as if
"Broderick Crawford should come bustling out of
it" (128), a reference to the old Highway Patrol
television series. Elsewhere, readers are invited
to visualize Esther Williams movies, "The Incred-
ible Hulk" episodes, and specific films: George A.
Romero's Night of the Living Dead and Dawn of the
Dead, and Ralph Bakshi's The Lord of the Rings.
Similar allusions occur in virtually every one of
King's major narratives, justifying in part Gray's
comments on the cinematic, visual effects in
King's prose.

One of the primary criticisms leveled against
The Talisman, in fact, was that it read like a

10

novelization for a film (Leerhsen 61). Leerhsen interprets that criticism negatively, apparently ignoring King´s frequent cinematic references and techniques (and, for that matter, Straub´s as well). Intensely visual imagery and use of films and television as structural devices, metaphors, similes, symbolic equivalents, or allusions enhancing the narrative do not make a work merely a novelization or its style essentially "postliterate." They may in fact emphasize the nature of the novel as a popular form inextricably allied to the visual arts. As Leon Edel says, "Novelists have sought almost from the first to become a camera . . . . A great anomaly in the history of painting and fiction is that the painters tried very hard to get away from the camera, where the novelists sought by every possible means to embrace it" (177, 178).

What we see in King, then, is a novelist closer than most to the visual arts, incorporating film references into his prose, structuring episodes on filmic techniques, and drawing on his readers´ reservoir of images from film and television.

In addition, King´s works illustrate the relationship Fiedler suggests between novel and cinema, if for no other reason than that so many of King´s stories have become films. David Schow´s discussion of King´s films concentrates on the disadvantages accruing to King from having his works filmed so frequently. Even the title, "Return of the Curse of the Son of Mr. King: Book Two," implicitly criticizes the tendency for horror films to spawn sequels, regardless of quality. And, as Schow indicates, the dangers King faces increase as each novel leads to "The imperative that best-sellers automatically insure box-office hits, and that the critical criteria for shooting such films down seems to amplify in proportion to the success the film enjoys" (49). When a King novel is optioned for film, it seems obvious to some that the book was intended all along as a film property and is therefore in some obscure way less than a novel. When the film diverges from the original (as almost all have), the same voices argue that because the films was flawed, the novel must have been also. For King, it is a no-win situation.

This tension largely arises among readers and viewers who misunderstand the relationship between novel and film. Anyone who has waited breathlessly for the film version of a favorite novel, only to be disappointed by the visual representation, has experienced the disparity between the two modes. Frank Herbert's <u>Dune</u> comes readily to mind; only viewers who had read the novel could follow the fragmented, allusive narrative--but those viewers would also be most sensitive to the enormous alterations imposed by the director, the actors, the set designers, etc.

Fiedler and Edel to the contrary on this point, novel <u>does</u> differ markedly from film. The novelist may try to re-create the visual effects of film, but cannot do so fully, just as the film-maker may attempt to re-create the texture of prose but must certainly fail. On the other hand, each genre includes specific strengths that sets it apart.

Seymour Chatman's "What Novels Can Do That Films Can't (and Vice Versa)" explores some seminal differences. The study of narrative, or "narratology," has determined that narrative consists of a "deep structure" that emerges independently from the medium expressing it. In other words, a narrative is simply a way of organizing text. That organization entails writing for stories and novels; spoken words and movements for actors; stylized sets imitating places for drama and film; movement for narrative ballet and mime; and music for such programmatic pieces as Prokofiev's <u>Peter and the Wolf</u>. The surface forms differ; the underlying story remains intact.

In order to accommodate to differing surface structures, narrative depends upon what Chatman defines as a dual time structure: plot time, or the time of the story itself; and discourse time, or the time involved in presenting the story. All narratives incorporate this dual sequence; and since the sequences operate independently of each other, they allow the same "story" to be expressed through a variety of media. Daniel Keyes can explore the consequences of a retarded character's rapid mental growth through a short story, "Flowers for Algernon"; a novella, "Flowers for Algernon"; a novel, <u>Flowers for Algernon</u>; or a film, <u>Charly</u> (1968). The representations change radic-

12

ally; the "story" remains the same. Thus, because of the dual time sequence, narrative is "translatable" from one medium to another.

When novelists interrupt the narrative flow with description, for example, story time stops but narrative time continues; for the moment, characters freeze. A film may "tell" the same story, but since it provides descriptions visually and immediately, it need not stop either plot time or discourse time. Both time structures proceed simultaneously.

On the other hand, because a film cannot stop plot time as easily as a narrative can, it becomes difficult for a film to develop intricate symbolic or imagistic patterns based on description. In King's The Shining, for example, much of the novel's power derives from Jack Torrance's consciously symbolic memories of such images as wasps. King frequently embeds patterns into his text, with plot time stopping to allow Jack page after page in which to define for himself (and for the reader) the symbolic values of things and events. In Kubrick's film, such stops would be impossible; the intricate pattern of painting imagery, color-coded rooms, or references to twelves which Thomas Allen Nelson discusses in Kubrick: Inside a Film Artist's Maze--or even the maze image itself--is largely inaccessible to viewers not present on the film's set or intimately aware of visual symbolology developed throughout Kubrick's films (197-231).

Even in as strongly a symbolic film as Lord of the Flies, the few seconds devoted to the flies buzzing around the impaled head of a dead pig stretch interminably, yet the same image in William Golding's novel creates a pivotal symbolic and thematic moment. The difference is simply that Golding can take the time to establish and explore the symbols; the film cannot. Similarly, in his version of The Shining, Kubrick deletes references to wasps, as critical as they are in the novel, substituting instead a symbol that functions on a different level. The maze is inherently visual and can be represented directly on film; it does not require that characters freeze during the discourse time in order to explain its significance.

In The Dead Zone, a similar difficulty occurs

13

in defining symbolic values. The novel focuses on
the Wheel of Fortune as image, and devotes several
passages to intellectualized considerations of the
image as symbol. Cronenberg´s film replaces an
essentially intellectual image with a visual one--
the roller coaster. The functions of the images
remain the same, even communicating many of the
same values; the forms differ, however, as novel
is adapted into cinema.

There is in addition a third level of "time"
defining differences between novel and film: perception time, or the time readers/viewers need to
apprehend the narrative--the actual reading ·time
for a novel or watching time for a film.

In King´s case, this third temporal consideration is unusually important. Part of the attrac-
tion of King´s novels stems from their ability to
create the illusion of a reality into which
something irrational and patently non-realistic
intrudes. Many of the stylistic techniques King
is noted for contribute directly to this sense.
Certainly the reference to brand-names and contemporary consumer goods helps, as does the simplicity of the style itself. Readers do not notice
King´s narrative style, as they might in reading
mainstream or "literary" novels; instead, they
move directly through a transparent style to engage the narrative head on. King calls his
writing the literary equivalent of a Big Mac and a
large order of fries; restated in critical termi-
nology, his writing subsumes considerations of
style to considerations of story. Reading King is
like hearing someone tell a good tale, a point
demonstrated for me several years ago when I heard
King read the then-unpublished "Mrs. Todd´s
Shortcut" at the International Conference on the
Fantastic in the Arts; voice and text blended
perfectly. The story became an extension of the
storyteller himself.

As a result, readers are almost bound to be
disappointed in film versions of the novels.
Carrie comes the closest to satisfying in this
respect, in part because it is King´s sparsest,
most streamlined novel; even there, however, the
decision to excise the documentary sense implicit
in the novel and replace it with overt, visceral
horror makes watching the film a different experience than reading the novel. With The Shining,

14

Salem's Lot (in spite of its mini-series format
extending over two nights); Firestarter, and
others, the disparities increase in proportion to
the original length of the novels. And the problem
can only get worse; The Stand and The Talisman
develop a grandeur simply through their sheer
mass; to reach the same sense in three or four
hours of viewing time is patently impossible. On
the other hand, the quickness of narrative in
"Children of the Corn," the sense of rapid movements irrevocably set into motion, dissipates in
the over-blown, full-length feature version;
speeches, scenes, whole episodes seem contrived
simply to fill up necessary minutes.

A final point that deserves mention here is
that the differentiation between novel and film
becomes even more pronounced in certain genres,
specifically fantasy and science fiction. In verbal form, both deal with the imaginary, with ex-
trapolative elements that do not have direct analogues in the objective world. As a result, the
readers are invited to--and in fact must--provide
most of the visualization themselves. It is one
thing for a reader to imagine Barlow and respond
as Straub did: "My God! I thought: a vampire!"
(8); it is quite another to have an external interpretation of what that character looks like
imposed upon a viewer. The fact that Tobe Hooper
elected to work with the older Nosferatu tradition, already fully developed in F. W. Murnau's
1922 silent film, rather than with the more
traditional Bela Lugosi/Frank Langella interpretation, alienated a number of viewers from the television version of Salem's Lot.

David J. Schow asks whether "written horror
can ever be faithfully translated from one medium
to another" (49), highlighting the underlying
question this volume intends to explore. In a
slightly different context, Allen Lichtenstein
argues that in the specialized case of science
fiction, the audiences for films and the audiences
for novels are not in fact the same. Citing
Thomas R. Atkins, Lichtenstein argues that the
differences between novel and film are so extreme
that they invite almost opposite reactions;
reading science fiction books touches the reader
at the intellectual level, while the science
fiction film (on the level of Star Wars and Close

15

<u>Encounters of the Third Kind</u> evokes "a more
visceral, adventure-oriented, and shared experience" (47). While Atkins and Lichtenstein speak
directly to science fiction, much the same is true
of dark fantasy and horror. While novels such as
<u>Carrie</u>, ´<u>Salem´s Lot</u>, <u>The Shining</u>, <u>The Dead Zone</u>
and others do entail a certain element of visceral
horror, they also invite intellectual responses;
the presence of cinematic allusions, for instance,
requires a certain degree of intellectualization
in reading the text. The films, on the other
hand, frequently subordinate that element to the
visual, visceral horror: the blood-stained hand
rising from the grave of the White house in de
Palma´s <u>Carrie</u>; floods of blood erupting from the
elevator in Kubrick´s <u>The Shining</u>; close-up shots
of Frank Dodd´s suicide in Cronenberg´s <u>The Dead
Zone</u>.

And thus the difficulty for readers and
viewers. Film versions of King´s novels are
almost guaranteed to follow with, as Schow puts
it, "bloodhound sureness." And they are equally
almost guaranteed to be as controversial as their
sources are popular. In part, that tension arises
from the natures of the two forms themselves--in
spite of close affinities, novel and film are not
the same, cannot represent the same deep-structure
of narrative identically. When the novel version
is by a leading fantasist, has enjoyed a tenure of
several months on multiple bestsellers lists, and
has garnered a solid core of dedicated fans, the
film can only hope to succeed by providing, not a
better experience, but a different one.

In his review of <u>Different Seasons</u>, Thomas
Gifford attempted to describe the tone and style
of that book. He struggled through an assessment
of King as storyteller--as "the storyteller his
readers would want to be if they were indeed
storytellers"--before arriving at his final approach:

> Wait. Let me try again. I think
> I´ve got it. Think of Stephen King and
> Steven Spielberg: work on that simple
> equation. One with words, the other
> with images. Elemental story values.
> Broad strokes. You begin to grasp an
> explanation of both phenomena. <u>E.T.</u>,

> _Poltergeist_, _Close Encounters_, _Jaws_,
> _Carrie_, _The Shining_, _Cujo_ . . . _Raiders_
> _of the Lost Ark_, _Different Seasons_. (2)

Although made over three years ago, Gifford´s conclusions remain valid. King´s novels _do_ exhibit
extraordinary affinities with film, while simultaneously retaining their identity as individual
approaches to narrative.

CHAPTER II

On the Nature of Horror

In "Special Make-up Effects and the Writer,"
King speaks about the relation between novelist
and filmmaker, with special attention on the central characteristic of horror:

> I'll show you things beyond your
> wildest dreams.
>   For a writer of novels--particular-
> ly spooky ones--showing the reader such
> wild things comes so cheap it's posi-
> tively disgusting. THE SHINING cost
> roughly 19 million dollars to produce as
> a film; it cost roughly $24.00 to pro-
> duce as a novel--costs of paper, type-
> writer ribbons, and postage. The thing
> is, when it's on the page it's what
> Paddy Cheyefsky once called "mental
> work" . . . and you can't put a price on
> that. (6)

Although the passage seems partially tongue-in-
cheek, it carries the weight of truth. The horror
novelist and the horror filmmaker have a common
goal: to generate a specific response in their
readers/viewers. And they share a number of techniques in reaching that goal.
    Along with other critics and writers, King
has investigated the nature of horror in fiction
and in film. In July 1982, King opened his review
of The Boogens by defining what horror (especially
the horror film) is not:

> It isn't just "kind" of a relief;
> it is a distinct relief. It isn't a
> message movie disguised as a horror
> movie (Wolfen), not some intellectual
> director's attempt to "rise above the
> genre" (The Shining, Ghost Story), not a
> snuff film disguised as a horror movie

(<u>Maniac</u>).

It´s--gasp--an "old-fashioned pretty good low-budget" horror movie. ("Digging <u>The Boogens</u>" 9)

Hidden beneath King´s typical colloquialisms and
authorial intrusions lie two important points:
that there is such a thing as a "horror film"; and
that it can be defined.

Other writers and reviewers have attempted to
do precisely that. J. P. Telotte approaches Val
Lewton´s <u>Isle of the Dead</u>, for example, through a
series of generalizations about the horror film.
Most such films, Telotte argues,

place the viewer within a realm that is
deceptively quotidian, and through a
series of jolting encounters with previ-
ously unseen terrors, they suggest a
need for greater awareness and caution
as one goes about his daily affairs.
(119-129)

The presence of a creature or monster catalyzes
characters´ responses to their world, simultaneously allowing the characters to adapt and cope to
the unreal or irrational.

Telotte sees horror as allied to reality,
with the horror mythos serving a deep-seated need
to "account for that which defies explanation, and
so render it less threatening to the human commun-
ity," a process which involves "mythic thinking"
(120). Such a process

admits man´s limitations, acknowledging
that the most fundamental mysteries
really lie <u>within</u>, sourced in the psyche
itself. It, therefore, affords a basic
means of dealing with that monstrous
presence, more precisely the absence or
void which lies at the center of the
self, upwelling from time to time to
remind us of how tentative our place in
the world remains. (120)

In the face of the rationality inherent in Western
society, the horror film reasserts the external
unknown, the mythic and mysterious intrusion that

19

requires control and threatens destruction. In
combining the two divergent forces, Telotte concludes, Lewton´s films touch upon "the essence of
the genre":

> they conjure a vision of those most ele-
> mental and powerful forces in man and
> his world which, despite our modern ef-
> forts, still deny appeasement and dis-
> concertingly confront us with our very
> human limits. (121)

To give a second, more concrete example, W.
H. Rockett discusses "The Door Ajar: Structure and
Convention in Horror Films That Would Terrify." He
begins by citing King´s contention in <u>Danse Maca-
bre</u> that "Nothing is so frightening as what´s
behind the closed door" (131; <u>DM</u> 114), then turning that dictum against King by arguing that to
open the door, while almost mandatory, deflates
the horror. The image of the door is revealing,
since, as Rockett indicates, showing a door implies that someone will open it: "Anything must be
fully realized, our natural and cultivated in-
clination tells us; in dramatic narratives, that
means an Aristotelian wholeness" (131).
Yet the true value of a story that would terrify, Rockett continues, depends upon the degree
to which the storyteller can withstand the pres-
sure to open the door and reveal the terror.
Again using King as a counter-argument, Rockett
contends that King´s argument in <u>Danse Macabre</u> and
the logic underlying it are fallacious. King
writes that "Human consciousness can deal with almost anything" (<u>DM</u> 114); Rockett claims that

> Movies and novels by their very nature
> cannot deliver something with which hu-
> man consciousness cannot cope, while the
> most horrible thing the author or the
> special effects man can whomp up can
> never match what lies beyond the thresh-
> hold of our imaginations. (132)

Beyond the closed door, the Ultimate Horror can
exist; once the door is opened, it "becomes fi-
nite," one of many horrifying things but no longer
Ultimate. It joins elements from the evening

news, headlines from magazines and newspapers, images from countless other horror films, and by doing so becomes diffuse and ceases to horrify.

The solution, Rockett says, is to follow Lovecraft and encourage the readers or viewers to accept a suspension of natural law and the intrusion of uncontrolled chaos--in Rockett's words, "knocking the stuffing out of Aristotelian plotting" (132). The structures which accommodate this approach use two techniques to create an imbalance in the viewer: relative closure of visual image and of plot; and violation of the norms of the horror genre itself.

In a visual sense, relative closure simply means obscuring part of the screen, thereby emphasizing what can be seen. Transferred to plot, it means inviting the closing ambiguities of such films as Carpenter's re-make of The Thing. In the Hawks/Nyby original, there is no question that the creature is dead; Carpenter, on the other hand, uses relative closure to create the most ambiguous conclusion possible: either survivor might be the thing, or neither, or both. In terms of visual relative closure, however, Rockett points out that James Arness' barely glimpsed creature is generally "more terrifying, if less horrifying" than the gelatinous monster Carpenter shows in so many close-ups. Rockett would thus presumably approve of the final scenes of De Palma's Carrie, Kubrick's The Shining, George A. Romero's Creepshow, or Daniel Attias' Silver Bullet, with their inherent indeterminacy and visual suggestions of horror continuing beyond death. Alternatively, he might disapprove of (or see as less effective) Cronenberg's The Dead Zone, which concludes with Johnny Smith's death and the restoration of order from chaos; or Cat's Eye, with its Lassie-like conclusion as the family stands around the grisly remains of the troll.

Rockett's second criteria--that effective horror films transcend their own generic conventions--is more easily demonstrated. He gives as an example The Howling, which transmutes traditional werewolf lore, specifically the belief that the creatures require night and the full moon to change or that they are tortured souls in the guise of beasts. The convention that sanctuary is inviolable is contravened in films such as The

21

<u>Exorcist</u> and <u>The Amityville Horror</u>. Here Rockett
points to King´s <u>´Salem´s Lot</u> as additional evidence (135); were he writing today, he might also
allude to <u>Silver Bullet</u>, with its contention that
Lowe can change at any time but prefers the full
moon because then the beast-part is more fully in
control.

These two devices--structural relative closure and violation of conventions--allow the
horror filmmaker to go beyond merely defining the
fantastic. Eric S. Rabkin´s 180° reversal is not
sufficient, Rockett contends:

> the horror filmmaker who would terrify
> goes even further then: not only does he
> present the audience with the new uni-
> verse for which they´ve contracted, one
> in which the ground rules of the normal
> world are turned upside down, but he
> also turns over selectively some of the
> conventional grounds rules of the genre
> itself. (135)

When it comes to King specifically, one can
approach the question from two directions: by
looking at what critics have said about films made
from King´s fictions and thereby adducing a theory
of horror film; and by seeing what King himself
has said about the genre.

Since many of the comments made about King´s
films will find their logical place in discussions
of individual works, it might suffice here to
point to comments such as David J. Schow´s that
King´s approach to horror fiction requires more
subtlety than many filmmakers are willing to provide. His fiction, Schow argues, is "a nether-
world apart from the self-renewing cycle of hor-
ror/gore epics that form the staple of the rural
drive-in circuit," requiring instead "filmmakers
with senses of craft, art, and humor that encom-
passes more than the needs of the cash till" (49).
Of the three films that Schow discusses, however,
only one--<u>Carrie</u>--approaches the sophistication
Schow requires of an effective horror film.

In talking about film versions of fiction by
Harold Pinter, Ernest Hemingway, Ray Bradbury, and
King, Harlan Ellison comments that while all four
seem to write on a straightforwardly accessible

level, they are in fact allegorical writers; each

> draws deeply from the well of myth and
> archetype. The collective unconscious
> calls to us and we go willingly where
> Hemingway and Bradbury and Pinter . . .
> and King beckon us to follow.
> Stephen King's books work as well
> as they do, because he is writing more
> of shadow than of substance. He drills
> into the flow of cerebro-spinal fluid
> with the dialectic function of a modern
> American mythos, dealing with archetypal
> images from the pre-conscious or con-
> scious that presage crises in our cul-
> ture even as they become realities.
> ("Part Two" 4)

The subsequent films, Ellison contends, ignore the
mythic qualities to concentrate on the immediacies
of horror and, as a result, fail to attain the
same sense of engagement with viewers.

Even more helpful at this juncture, however,
is to discover what King himself has said about
the nature of horror films.

Most of his earlier comments have appeared in
Stephen King's Danse Macabre (1981), his critical
study of horror fiction and film. The book includes several chapters on film: "The Modern
American Horror Movie--Text and Subtext," "The
Horror Movie as Junk Food," and, concentrating on
television, "The Glass Teat, or, This Monster Was
Brought to You by Gainesburgers." Available in
hardcover and trade paperback editions, Danse Macabre is enjoyable, less an academic text than a
personal history of King's involvement with the
genre, written in King's colloquial style, stopping along the way for biographical profiles of
major figures, plot summaries of old favorites,
and popularized critical analyses of purposes and
effects.

Parts of Danse Macabre were excerpted and reprinted as magazine articles, including "Why We
Crave Horror Movies" (Playboy, January 1981; a
version of "The Modern American Horror Movie");
"Notes on Horror" (Quest, June 1981; a heavily revised version of "October 4, 1957, and an Invita-
tion to Dance"); and "You Gotta Put on the

Gruesome Mask and Go Booga-Booga" (TV Guide 5 December 1981; a version of "The Glass Teat"). In each, he discusses horror film as creating a liaison between between the real and the unreal, providing a social barometer for "those things that trouble the night thoughts of a whole society" ("Why We Crave" 150), and as forming an outlet for fears and aggressions that might otherwise become a disruptive force. After an afternoon in a dark movie-house watching vampires or werewolves or assorted other masters of mayhem, he argues, the real world seems paradoxically less threatening, more orderly after the chaos of film. "It is very difficult to write a successful horror story in a world that is so full of real horrors," King writes in "You Gotta Put on the Gruesome Mask":

> A ghost in the turret room of a Scottish castle just cannot compete with thousand megaton warheads or nuclear-power plants that apparently have been put together from Aurora model kits by 10-year-olds with poor eye-hand coordination. Still horror can be done . . . . (65)

In addition to his theoretical statements, King· has provides practical guidelines for what he considers effective horror films. The "Garbage Truck" columns refer to a number of films: The Attack of the Giant Leeches, listed among his favorite films (21 May 1970); The Creature from the Black Lagoon (29 March 1969); Dracula (19 February 1970); Frankenstein (19 February 1970); The Haunting, based on Shirley Jackson´s The Haunting of Hill House (19 February 1970); Psycho (27 June 1969, 18 July 1969, 19 February 1970); and The Werewolf (18 July 1969).

Nearly a decade later, in the December 27, 1979 issue of Rolling Stone, King published "The Horrors of ´79," a lengthy discussion of the state of filmmaking at the end of the decade. Among the horror films (or films incorporating horror) he mentions as being particularly strong are George A. Romero´s Dawn of the Dead, the long-awaited sequel to Night of the Living Dead; Francis Ford Coppola´s Apocalypse Now, with Marlon Brando´s rendition of Conrad´s "The horror, the horror"; Phantasm, boasting a demon wrecking ball; Night-

24

wing, which he considers "the cheerful Hollywood ruination of a really good novel"; De Palma's <u>The Fury</u>; Carpenter's <u>Halloween</u>; and <u>Alien</u>, which includes "H. R. Giger's alien, surely the most frightening film creature of the decade." Of the latter he adds that

> There are only two scenes in recent memory that match the moment when the alien comes bursting out of that hapless fellow's stomach at the dinner table: one occurs when the dead black man takes a chomp out of his wife's shoulder in <u>Dawn of the Dead</u>; the other comes in William Friedkin's <u>The Exorcist</u>, when Linda Blair's head does a complete 360, as the race drivers put it. (17)

The most important of the films, as far as King is concerned, however, is Romero's <u>Dawn of the Dead</u>, with King speaking of Romero arguably "<u>the</u> director of the Seventies; even more than Coppola, he gives us that exciting sense of a unified vision, an idea dovetailing neatly with creative bent and emotional commitment" as he works through "total chaos" to an image of sense (18).

An article for <u>TV Guide</u> called simply "Horrors!" (30 October 1982), engages in pragmatic popular criticism by simply listing King's choices for the scariest horror films available on videocassette, along with a brief justification for each. Starting from the least scary, the list includes:

1. George A. Romero's <u>Night of the Living Dead</u> (1968);
2. <u>An American Werewolf in London</u> (1981);
3. Don Siegel's <u>Invasion of the Body Snatchers</u> (1956);
4. Howard Hawks' <u>The Thing</u> (1951);
5. <u>The Shining</u> (1980), noted for its "claustrophobic terror";
6. <u>Rabid</u> (1977), directed by David Cronenberg
7. <u>Wolfen</u> (1980), based on Whitley Strieber's novel;
8. <u>Dead of Night</u> (1945);

    9. Carpenter´s <u>The Fog</u> (1980);
   10. <u>The Toolbox Murders</u> (1978).

Three years later, <u>USA Today</u> published a similar
article, "Stephen King: His Creepiest Movies" (27
August 1985), in which King revised and updated
his list of the "top" five: <u>The Evil Dead</u> (1983),
<u>Night of the Living Dead</u> (1968), <u>Let´s Scare Jes-
sica to Death</u> (1971), <u>Alien</u> (1979), and <u>The Haunt-
ing</u> (1963).
    While lists such do not constitute a canon of
critical standards, they do indicate what King
considers models for horror films to follow. Even
without an extensive review of <u>Danse Macabre</u>, for
example, it is possible to begin working out what
King expects. Add to that a few other articles,
including "Market Writer and the Ten Bears," with
its list of ten standard "horrors"; "How To Scare
a Woman To Death"; "Digging <u>The Boogens</u>"; and "<u>The
Evil Dead</u>: Why You Haven´t Seen It Yet . . . and
Why You Ought To"--and it becomes clear what King
considers an effective, viable horror film.
    But there is one additional ingredient, one
which should not be ignored in any discussion of
King´s fiction or the films made from it. In
"Digging <u>The Boogens</u>," King comments that what he
enjoyed most in the film was its "extravagant,
all-out embrace of what may be fantasy´s most lib-
erating statement: ´<u>I</u> don´t have to explain this;
<u>you</u> explain this.´" The result is a "wildly ener-
getic, often comic monster movie" that meets the
ultimate criterion for King: "horror movies were
always supposed to be <u>fun</u>, damn it, <u>fun</u>, and when
I left the theater after <u>The Boogens</u> that´s how I
felt . . . as if I´d had <u>fun</u>" (10).
    That may be the ultimate criterion in assess-
ing King´s films as well. After 1982--the year
in which he published both "Digging <u>The Boogens</u>"
and "<u>The Evil Dead</u>"--King became more involved in
filmmaking. In 1982, <u>Creepshow</u> appeared, a collaboration between King and Romero. In 1985, <u>Cat´s
Eye</u> and <u>Silver Bullet</u> were produced, both from
King´s screenplays. His directorial debut came
almost simultaneously, with <u>Overdrive</u>, scheduled
for release in July, 1986.
    For the first time, then, King had control
over what films made from his fictions would look
like. More and more, they reflect his unique ap-

proach to the horror film as a genre . . . and as vehicle for pure, straightforward fun.

King's "presence" in films made from his novels and stories has become a critical element determining responses to those films. It has become a commonplace that a King novel will reach the national bestsellers lists and subsequently become a film--if not a box-office smash, then at least a respectable draw. Of the major novels published to 1983, only <u>The Stand</u> has not yet made it to the screen; film and media magazines are replete, however, with interviews in which King discusses the status of his screenplay for that novel. The works published since 1983--<u>Pet Sematary</u> and <u>The Talisman</u>--have been optioned or are in progress. And one can only assume that <u>The Eyes of the Dragon</u>, <u>It</u>, <u>Misery</u>, and <u>The Tommyknockers</u> will receive the same treatment when they receive mass-market publication. While film production may not be as expeditious as it was for <u>Christine</u>, which began filming four days before the novel's publication (Zoglin), it seems a reasonable guess that all four will eventually become film properties, along with a number of stories now available in <u>Skeleton Crew</u>.

Yet, perhaps not surprisingly, few of the films made from King's fictions have attained the drawing power of their originals. Some generated immediate and negative criticism. <u>Children of the Corn</u> was more embarrassment than effective film experience, for example, while one television reviewer passed over <u>Silver Bullet</u> as "garbage." Other films, however, retained both the essence of King's unique vision and their integrity as films. In spite of having been released within five months of each other and having contributed to the sarcastically named King film-of-the-month club mentioned by several critics, <u>Cujo</u>, <u>The Dead Zone</u>, and <u>Christine</u> performed respectably, both cinematically and economically. And, while none of the films has yet become a box-office smash, every one since De Palma's <u>Carrie</u> in 1976 has at least cleared expenses and made a profit (Zoglin).

The reactions of King's readers and critics to the films vary widely. On one side, King's enormous popularity as a writer almost guarantees marginal success for any film associated with him; simple curiosity might create enough interest for

a film to break even. Consequently, as Zoglin
says, "Hollywood seems ready to snap up virtually
anything King sets to paper short of his grocery
list--and there is no guarantee some enterprising
director will not put <u>that</u> on celluloid some dark
and stormy night."

On the other side stand readers and viewers
who find Kubrick´s re-visualization of <u>The Shining</u>
offensive, or Tobe Hooper´s <u>Salem´s Lot</u> simply
boring. Bill Munster, the editor of <u>Footsteps</u>,
recently assessed the films from his own perspective of what constituted an effective King film:

> For me the only decent film made of
> King´s work has been <u>Carrie</u>--and that´s
> it! <u>The Shining</u> was Kubrick annoying us
> with all his cinematic bull-shit;
> <u>Salem´s Lot</u> was hopelessly television
> from opening to closing: <u>Christine</u> a big
> nothing; <u>Firestarter</u> was too funny for
> words and clearly miscast--I was waiting
> for Art Carney to go into his Ed Norton
> at any minute: <u>Cat´s Eye</u> a bit too glib;
> <u>Children of the Corn</u> deserves to send
> all those who purchased tickets an
> apology; <u>Creepshow</u>, better than the
> rest; <u>Cujo</u> had potential but lost it:
> and the <u>Dead Zone</u> another treat, much in
> the same boat as <u>Carrie</u> (Letter, 6
> October 1985).

Each film, it seems, has its advocates and
detractors; often the discussion over relative
merits is as heated as discussions of the novels
themselves. In a recent survey, <u>Castle Rock</u> asked
its readers to name their favorites. At the top
was <u>The Dead Zone</u>, followed by <u>Cujo</u>, <u>Creepshow</u>,
<u>The Shining</u>, and <u>Carrie</u>. In sixth place was
<u>Christine</u>, with <u>Firestarter</u> and <u>Salem´s Lot</u> tied
for eighth and ninth, and <u>Cat´s Eye</u> pulling up
tenth--an arrangement that will seem perfectly
fine for many viewers and skewed to others.

Further complicating matters are King´s responses to the films. From the beginning, he has
dissociated himself from many of the finished
products, arguing that no matter how abysmal a
film adaptation may be, it cannot alter the words
of the book on the shelf; the novel will endure

unchanged regardless. While that seems a healthy attitude to take (particularly in light of producers´ and directors´ demonstrated disinclination until recently to work from King´s adaptations of his works), it also hides an implicit danger. "Children of the Corn" was a finely wrought, powerful short story; the film version missed on almost every count. And, unfortunately, among those viewing the film would be those who had not yet read the story, who had come--perhaps to their first King film--out of curiosity to see what this King fellow was all about. Their attitudes will be based on the film, not the story, and King´s reputation may suffer for it.

As far as the films themselves go, King has said continually that he feels at least comfortable with most. As he said in an interview with Craig Modderno,

> I don´t feel good or bad about them. I liked Cujo very much. I liked Carrie very much . . . . I liked Cat´s Eye. It really works, and I´m sort of disappointed that it´s not doing any better. . . .
> A lot of the other ones are just sort of not there. None of them are really bad. None of them are really embarrassing, although Children of the Corn is pretty bad. Firestarter missed by just an inch of being a picture like Myra Breckenridge or Mommy Dearest. But it didn´t happen.

His attitudes toward particular films have, of course, altered over the years; but perhaps the best (and certainly among the most recent) summation of King´s responses appears in an interview recorded by Tyson Blue on the set of Overdrive and published in Castle Rock (November 1985). When asked if there was some particular thing he wanted to do as director, King answered, "Yeah. To try and tell the story that´s between the lines." By that, he explains, he means the essence--the special "something" that is Stephen King and that underlies all of his printed words. In some of the films, he continues,

29

there is a trace of what I do.   There´s
some of it in "Children of the Corn."
And there´s a lot of it in "Cujo."   But
there´s no Stephen King in "Firestarter." And it´s very faithful to the
book, but it´s just that--I´m not in
that movie at all, whatever it was that
was in the book that people liked.

His stated purpose in directing <u>Overdrive</u>, then,
is to try translating that ineffable "something,"
that essential element that distinguishes Stephen
King´s fictions from all others. Perhaps in <u>Over-
drive</u>, for the first time, viewers will enjoy an
ideal balance of components: horror film, King
narrative, and visual interpretation.

CHAPTER III

Carrie (1976)

During an interview with King in 1978, Peter S. Perakos asked King about Brian De Palma´s film version of Carrie. He liked it, King responded, adding that

> The attitude of the film was different
> from my book; I tended to view the e-
> vents straight-on, humorlessly, in a
> straight point-to-point progression (you
> have to remember that the genesis of
> Carrie was no more than a short story
> idea), while I think De Palma saw a
> chance to make a movie that was a satir-
> ical view of high school life in general
> and high school peer-groups in particu-
> lar.
>   In the book, Carrie destroyed the
> entire town on the way home: that didn´t
> happen in the movie, mostly because the
> budget was too small. I wish they could
> have had that, but otherwise, I don´t
> have any real quibbles. I think that De
> Palma is a worthy pretender to Hitch-
> cock´s throne . . . certainly he is as
> peculiar as Hitchcock. (14)

Responding to Janet Maslin´s criticism in Newsweek that the film incorporated elements of "offhand misogyny" and "studied triviality," King reiter- ated his point that both film and novel worked through the problems of isolation and ostracism, of In-groups and Out-groups. For King, at least, De Palma´s visions captured the essence of that struggle.

Other viewers and critics responded more openly to cinematic allusions throughout the film, concentrating in particular on De Palma´s debt to Alfred Hitchcock. Janet Lorenz attributes many characteristics of the film to similarities "of

31

style rather than of plot" between Hitchcock and
De Palma, mentioning parallels between shots of
Carrie in the gym shower and Janet Leigh's famous
shower scene in Psycho. The high school has been
re-named Bates High School, a reference to Norman
Bates. And, Lorenz concludes, Pino Donaggio's
score often echoes Bernard Hermann's Psycho theme
(408-410).

Leigh A. Ehlers goes even further; the film,
Ehlers notes, elicited comments by reviewers about
De Palma's "emulation" of Hitchcock in Obsession
and Carrie; a footnote cites Bruce Kawin's comment
about "blatant references" to Psycho, although
Kawin does not specify particulars. Still, there
is sufficient evidence to justify this approach to
the film.

Yet another approach concentrates on changes
between novel and film. As the first film made
from King's works, Carrie is tight, closer to the
text than Kubrick's The Shining, for example, yet
more vivid and full of life than Tobe Hooper's
Salem's Lot or Di Laurentiis's Firestarter. Even
so, there were a number of major alterations, the
most immediately apparent being a shift from a
documentary sense to overt visual romanticism.

A number of critics have worked with fairy
tale themes in King's novel, including Chelsea
Quinn Yarbro in "Cinderella's Revenge--Twists on
Fairy Tale and Mythic Themes in the Work of Stephen King" (FI), and Alex E. Alexander in "Stephen
King's Carrie--A Universal Fairy Tale." The fact
remains, however, that the text of King's novel
itself emphasizes a rationalist, non-fairy-tale
view of reality through its documentary pose. The
multiple perspectives of characters, reporters,
Congressional committees, and academics not only
recapitulate the nineteenth-century approach to
horror novels, such as Mary Shelley had used in
Frankenstein, but engage King in a dialogue with
his readers:

> By introducing a split narrative frame-
> work into his novel, King examines the
> human desire to explain phenomena, to
> digest and to rationalize reality. The
> dangers of a compartmentalized response
> to reality become apparent when put to
> the ultimate test--Carrie, or that which

is beyond previous experience. (Ehlers,
40)

As the various "sources" recount their experiences
or their conclusions, the readers must correlate
data and fact, sift through opinion and prejudice,
to discover the "true" Carrie White underlying all
--or perhaps to discover that they simply cannot
do so. The puzzle that is Carrie White may outwit
us all.

In De Palma's film, we lose much of that
sense. Instead, we see Carrie through the camera's eye, watching her in moments of fear, anger,
frustration, and crisis. We come to know her more
completely and more directly through Spacek's
nuances of movement than through anything said
about her by others. Even elements as apparently
minor as distorted camera angles emphasize
Carrie's isolation, wedding theme to technique.

Originally, however, the film was apparently
intended to parallel King's approach more closely.
The first draft of the screenplay, credited to
Larry Cohen and Paul Monash, transferred several
of King's novelistic techniques, including frequent flashbacks to Carrie's childhood and character development primarily through dialogue. The
opening shot of Carrie's house, initially striking
in its whiteness, was to grow more and more intense until the screen was filled with white,
suddenly cut to black for abbreviated credits, and
then just as suddenly cut to a close-up of Sue
Snell testifying before a panel of unseen investi-
gators. Following Sue's introductory remarks
about Carrie and Margaret White, the script called
for a flashback to Stella Horan's backyard and a
re-creation of the rain of stones.

In the second draft (January 1976), credited
to Cohen only, the opening dialogue has been
dropped; the scene cuts from a close-up shot of
the White house to Stella Horan's backyard--this
version of the film begins with flashback, which
continues as a central device throughout.

In this second draft, the conclusion has
altered radically as well. In the original version, Monash and Cohen followed King's ending,
with Carrie stopping Margaret White's heart; Sue
Snell arrives in time to be with Carrie at the
moment of her death. In the second, Carrie kills

33

her mother through telepathic manipulation of
kitchen utensils--but Sue Snell still arrives, and
confronts Carrie. When a rain of stones begins,
Carrie uses her telepathy to hurl Sue from the
house. Sue runs, turns, and watches the stones
pound the house into the ground. The final scene
reveals a vacant lot with a "FOR SALE" sign dis-
figured by the sentence "Carrie White is Burning
for Her Sins" and below it "Jesus Never Fails."
There is no suggestion of the famous (or infamous)
hand rising from the ashes, nor is Sue Snell
present.

In general, then, both early drafts reiterate
the pseudo-documentary sense of King's original.
We know Carrie either through Sue Snell and others
and their reactions to Carrie or through overt
flashbacks revealing the development of Carrie's
powers.

The film as finally produced, however,
clearly shifts from this secondary, documentary
sense. The opening scene gives a realistic view
of a girls' volleyball game at Bates High School
and underscores Carrie's isolation--but it fades
almost immediately into a shower scene at once
reminiscent of _Psycho_ and indicative of the
directions the film will follow. In a quick break
with realistic presentation, the camera follows
the girls through the locker room, recording their
actions (but not their voices) in slow motion and
soft-edged images. The scene becomes increasingly
sensual as the camera focuses on Carrie; then the
romantic flute music which had provided background
stops as Carrie sees the blood. The erotic sense
is destroyed as the film breaks back to reality,
with the girls' voices and Carrie's frantic "Help
me! Help me!"

From that point, the film continues the shift
from apparent realism to the fantastic, gradually
emphasizing horrific elements more and more. The
scene in Mr. Morton's office, for example, seems
straightforward enough, at least until the ashtray
shatters on the floor as a result of Carrie's
powers. Earlier in the scene, however, a bit of
editing connects the shower scene with the cata-
clysmic conclusion. In one shot, a fairly distant
shot of both Miss Collins and Mr. Morton, Collins's blue warmup jacket reaches to the hem of
her shorts, covering most of the material. Then

the camera cuts to a close-up of Morton's face. His eyes drop, focusing on Collins's shorts, which are fully visible: the jacket has disappeared, her blouse is tucked into the waistband, and Carrie's bloody fingerprints stain the pure whiteness of the shorts. Then the camera resumes an objective distance. Morton and Collins are standing as before--and her jacket again covers the bloody marks. Careful editing embeds an image of horror and a foreshadowing of what is to come into an ostensibly realistic scene.

Similar treatments occur throughout the film. In the scene in which Carrie shatters her bedroom mirror in her first conscious display of power, the glass fragments into shards and apparently falls to the floor; yet when Margaret enters to investigate the sounds, the mirror is cracked but otherwise intact--reflecting a distorted version of Carrie and of the nightlight Christ. De Palma explores the possibilities of reality, illusion, and manipulation of the viewer even more overtly in the scenes at the slaughterhouse. As Billy Nolan, Chris Hargensen, and the others approach the pens, De Palma treats the viewers to a panoramic shot of a stridently pastoral mural: cattle, pastures, blue skies with puffy white clouds (all adorning the Farmer John packing house in Los Angeles). Gradually, the mural becomes the background it at first pretends to be; when the actors reach the corner and the real pens and real pigs come into sight, the effect is virtually the same as the split-scene technique De Palma uses during the Prom scene. For an instant, the viewer is not sure which is real, which illusion; editing and camera angles emphasize the ambiguity, further confusing the lines between what is and what seems.

Still later, De Palma again blends realistic portrayals with illusion and fantasy. Tommy Ross and friends are trying on tuxedos--the more outrageous the better. To make explicit the comic elements in the scene, De Palma chooses to run the film at high speed, then to cut to Carrie methodically (and ineptly) trying lipsticks at a cosmetics counter. The rapid cutting back and forth, coupled with the high-speed chatter from Tommy and the others, reminds the viewer that what is happening on the screen is an illusion, shadows rather than reality, yet Carrie is caught within that illusion. For her, it has become real.

The Prom scene itself is an exercise in a similar ambiguity, based on a rapid transition from realism to starry-eyed, sentimentalized romanticism. Careful color treatments emphasize the fairy-tale sense of the Prom: Tommy Ross´s rather chaste-seeming blue car opposes Billy Nolan´s passionate red one, just as Ross´s chivalric treatment of Carrie as they sit outside the gym opposes Nolan´s cruelty toward Chris Hargensen earlier. Inside the gym, as Tommy Ross and Carrie dance, soft blue light sparkles from glitter-strewn cardboard stars and a mirror-ball, enhanced by the circling, waist-high camera angles that transform Carrie and Tommy into an idealized, romanticized couple. They circle faster and faster, obviously entranced with each other; the fantasy is complete.

At the climax approaches, the tension between realistic representation and fantastic image intensifies as well. As Carrie marks the fatal "X" on the ballot, the color wheel shifts to red. As Carrie and Tommy march forward to the accompaniment of romantic violin arpeggios and slow-motion shots, Tommy is highlighted by blue, Carrie by red . . . with a sudden cut to Chris and Billy beneath the platform. A ceiling shot shows the stage bathed in blue but the girders and bucket in startling red.

Carrie and Tommy stand crowned Queen and King. Chris pulls the rope, and the blood spills over Carrie. There is silence, except for the banging of the bucket, an irritating, realistic intrusion symbolizing the fragmentation of Carrie´s romantic illusion.

When De Palma shifts to split-screen, the erotic romanticism explicit in the shower scene and sublimated in the Prom scene disappears, replaced by a different kind of pseudo-documentary. We do not <u>hear</u> about the disaster; we <u>see</u> it. And even more critically, we see it simultaneously from multiple perspectives. Blue fades completely, replaced by red: the red of Carrie´s stained dress and the blood (more each time the camera returns to her); the red of inadequate lighting as bulbs burst; the red of flames; and finally the red blood of Carrie´s victims. Implicit threats become explicit action: in a scene not fully justified by the script (and denied in King's text), a beam, obviously directed by Carrie's telekinetic power, drops and kills Miss Collins. As Carrie leaves the gym, the splitscreen in turn disappears.

Another structural ambiguity develops during the final scenes. Carrie returns home and bathes, a careful re-creation of the initial shower scene. This time, however, the ritual cleansing under-scores the tragic irony of Carrie White. She literally bathes in blood, numbed by what has happened. Instead of soft-edged, romanticized shots against a white background (the shower tiles), we see clearly defined images against shadows—one of which conceals Margaret White. Instead of running naked to her peers, the outsider screaming for help and understanding, Carrie dresses in a vir-ginally white nightdress, embraces her mother, and cries "Please hold me," reversing the movement of the opening scene and making explicit once again the underlying theme of the film and of the novel: isolation.

The cinematic shifts and manipulations, in fact, parallel that theme throughout. Carrie does not belong—not to the solid, realistically pre-sented world of Bates High School, and not to the fantasy world of romantic illusion. She is, throughout, external to all around her, finally repudiated even by her own mother.

The central theme emerges as early as the opening scene: a volleyball game. Carrie misses the game point, losing the game for her team and their respect for herself. Her isolation becomes evident as the other girls push past her into the locker room. From that point on, De Palma empha-sizes her as the outsider. She becomes the object of the girls' ridicule in the shower scene. Cam-era angles distort her image in the principal's office and in her first confrontation with Margar-et White. Her tentative movement toward involve-ment—her comment on Tommy Ross's poem—is met with ridicule and criticism. She looks in at the punishment roll-call in the gym, unaware of the graffiti directed against her on the inside walls. Again and again, De Palma translates King's images into cinematic equivalents that define Carrie as the ultimate outsider; to that extent, the film

37

parallels not only King's Carrie but his earlier
novel Rage, a scathing attack on the internal
politics of American high schools and their hypo-
critical imposition of standards (and double
standards) upon adolescents (cf. Collings, SKRB
20-45).

At the end of the film, Carrie's ostracism is
complete. Everyone who has tried to help her has
been destroyed, physically or psychically. Miss
Collins had taken her aside earlier, urging her to
open up more; it is significant, however, that the
conversation takes place in an isolated part of
the school yard, away from others, with Carrie
literally cornered and set apart. In spite of
Miss Collins's concern--developed even further at
the Prom--she dies. Tommy Ross dies. And Sue
Snell suffers a mental breakdown perhaps worse
than death itself. Carrie White is not only an
outsider; she destroys any who attempt to break
down barriers between herself and normality.

Her isolation is, of course, a result of Margaret White's distorted religious fanaticism, in
De Palma's film a thinly disguised sexual repres-
sion tending to obsession. Even within the stark
framework of her home, with its miniature Gothic
arches, votive candles, and shrines, Carrie no
longer fits. Her discovery of her telekinetic
powers, which De Palma defines as a separate phenomenon from the mother's fanaticism, drives a
wedge between her and her mother. In the closing
scenes, Carrie returns home, rejected by the
outside world, only to be rejected by her inner
world as well; her mother, the one person who
should protect and understand her, stabs her.

In her fear and pain, Carrie strikes back,
crucifying her mother with kitchen utensils. Margaret White's death agonies are long and vocal,
blending ecstacy and passion until her cries are
barely distinguishable from those of orgasmic in-
tercourse. She recapitulates the pose of the crucifix in the closet, including the open, staring
eyes; and lest the audience miss the symbol, De
Palma focuses on Margaret's body, stopping the
action of the narrative and the film.

With Margaret's death, Carrie has pushed her
isolation as far as possible. She has killed
everyone who has touched her life, dissolving all
social bonds until there are literally no groups

left. At that moment, the final disaster strikes: the house itself, a continuing image of security for Carrie White, fragments--perhaps Carrie uses her powers to pull it in on herself and her mother's body. At any rate, she retreats to her sanctuary and the house burns around her, with De Palma again focusing on the statue, its eyes glowing, its hair in wild disarray. With her death, Carrie's isolation is complete.

Other characters are also isolated in the film. At first Chris Hargenson belongs to the in-group that includes Sue Snell. When Chris confronts Miss Collins, however, that group dissolves. "She can't get away with this if we all stick together," Chris cries, only to be ignored. The others turn their backs on her, setting her outside the group that has become her focus. In a later scene, Tommy Ross is running with the track team, the only one wearing black instead of orange; he differs physically as well as psychologically. Even a detail as apparently minor as hair correlates with this over-riding theme. Sue Snell, Tommy Ross, and Margaret White all share distinctive hair styles: curly verging on kinky, natural verging on wild. By itself, the style would be unremarkable; in conjunction with the figure in Carrie's closet, however, it seems more purposeful than accidental. The three central figures in Carrie's tragedy resemble the crucifix; all three suffer because of Carrie, and two die because of her.

The third, Sue Snell, does not die but is altered by her relationship with Carrie. The closing episode begins by suggesting the dreamy romanticism of the shower scene: soft-edged photography, violin music, slow-motion shots of blue skies and white picket fences. Dressed in white, Sue Snell approaches the remains of Carrie's home and lays a bouquet on the ashes--the flowers, by the way, continue the film's color symbolism: they are primarily red and white.

Then the bloody hand reaches up, grasping Sue's wrist and startling the audience. This conclusion is perhaps De Palma's clearest departure from King's text, and certainly the most problematical, since it seems external to the narrative. King approved of the interpolation, arguing that the scene emphasizes for viewers the extent to which _they_ have been manipulated by the film, a point Janet E. Lorenz repeats: "The final twist leaves us shaken and frightened, but our fear soon turns to amusement as we realize that this time the joke is on us" (410). In October, 1980, King participated with Ira Levin, Peter Straub, and George Romero in a round-table discussion of horror on The Dick Cavett Show. King refers to the scene in response to Cavett's question about how films and novels differ. "I think it's a Polanski film," Cavett says, "in which a character moves to the bathroom medicine chest mirror and just for an intance [sic] it registers that someone is standing in the room over here, and it gives me goose pimples when I think of it." Could King _write_ such a scene and get the same response from his readers?

> King: That thing I think you could. There are other things that I don't think you could do very effectively. There's that thing that De Palma does at the end of the film of Carrie, where the hand shoots out of the ground and grabs Amy Irving and--it's not in the book. And I think, if it was in the book, it would have nowhere near the effect that it has in the movie.

> Cavett: Reading the words, "Suddenly a hand shot out of the ground," is not as scary as--Or you'd have to do it another way, perhaps. It'd be an interesting exercise, wouldn't it?

> King: Exorcise. (9)

Here King identifies the primary effect of the scene: it is cinematic, rather than narrative. Even knowing what is to come, watching the film for the second or third or fourth time, viewers are still startled by the hand. And that is both the strength and the weakness of the conclusion. It startles; it does not terrify, horrify, or touch any emotions deeper than neural response. Intended as an image of indeterminacy, suggesting that the tragedy is not yet over, De Palma's scene remains unconnected with the film as a whole, a

single startling moment that the viewer antici-
pates but nonetheless succumbs to. Everything in
the final scene demands such a moment; the viewers
are waiting and watching, tensed and alert. And
even so, the bloody hand takes them unaware. The
technique has become almost standard in filming
King's novels: the revenant Susan Norton at the
conclusion of Salem's Lot; the presumably horrifying close-up of the photograph in the Overlook's
ballroom in Kubrick's The Shining; the rock music
and creaking metal at the end of Carpenter's
Christine; George's glowing eyes in "Gramma"; and
perhaps most inappropriately the final gasp of the
werewolf in Silver Bullet, even after the creature
has transformed back into the human. In each
instance, it is as if the directors were committed
to delivering a final chill, delaying the closing
credits until they have made one more attack upon
the viewers' nervous systems. Of them all, Carrie
succeeds most completely.

As a film translation of King's prose, Carrie
ranks among the best. Since the novel was itself
spare and concise, the film comes closer to the
major narrative threads. The documentary sense of
the novel helps the film in determining and
developing characters, while the casting led to
strong and believable characters. Sissy Spacek
and Piper Laurie do not physically resemble King's
Carrie and Margaret White but bring an intensity
to their roles that penetrates beneath the physical and re-creates the psychological. Secondary
characters are equally strong: Amy Irving, William
Katz (in spite of his occasionally distracting
hair style), and John Travolta as a charmingly
despicable Billy Nolan.

As the first film of a King novel, Carrie
brought King to public awareness. De Palma made
the film, King once commented, annd the film made
him. After the appearance of Carrie, Stephen King
was well on his way to becoming a household name
in horror.

CHAPTER IV

Salem's Lot (1979)

Salem's Lot stands unique among film versions of King's works.

First, it is to date the only feature film of a King novel made specifically for television. And second, it is so far the only King miniseries, and thus the only major film to have sufficient screen time to work in depth with King's multi-leveled narrative.

First optioned in 1975, after the appearance of Carrie but before the resounding success of De Palma's adaptation of that novel, Salem's Lot was originally scheduled for theatrical release. To that end, Warner Brothers began working on screen-play treatments; in the next two years, the studio rejected scripts by Stirling Silliphant, Robert Getchell, and Lawrence Cohen, and finally turned the project over to Warner Brothers Television.

Richard Kobritz, then executive production manager at Warner Brothers Television, undertook to complete the project himself, rejecting earlier screen treatments and deciding to produce the film as a two-night, four-hour mini-series (actually 3 1/2 hours plus commercial time). He hired Paul Monash, already associated with King through his screenplay for De Palma's Carrie, to write a new script directed to a television audience. The result, broadcast in November 1979, was the first appearance of a King novel on national television.

As a mini-series, the film was also the first to recognize a basic fact underlying almost all adaptations of King's works to film. Stephen King needs time. In a few instances, such as Children of the Corn, the narrative was not sufficient for the film time required; in others, notably The Woman in the Room, producers limited film-time to correspond with narrative simplicity. With Carrie, film-time and narrative-time were close, in part because Carrie was King's most compressed novel, with the narrative expanded by pseudo-documentary additions to lengthen it for publica-

42

tion as a novel. In almost every other case, however, the novel or story has proven too complex for limited treatment in two hours. With few exceptions, the film versions have suffered from the inevitable streamlining of plot, character, and narrative--a problem plaguing King's present attempts to transform The Stand into a film. Originally proposed as a two-part film, it is being pared down closer and closer to the three- to four-hour maximum conventionally allowable for feature films.

With Salem's Lot, such was not to be the case.

Unfortunately, however, Kobritz's plans were less successful than he might have hoped. For many viewers, the result was not four hours of Stephen King, but three-hours-plus of tedium. David Schow opens his assessment of the film by arguing that

> The only way a discussion of Salem's Lot can be prefaced is by the unhappy reality that television, as a medium for reaching a vast audience in an inexpensive way, is not only more subverted and restrictive than it was in the "less permissive" era of even two decades ago, but as a result now takes no chances; risks nothing. (50)

The film, he concludes, is simply boring.

Such a conclusion is particularly unfortunate in light of the extensive planning that went into the production. In interviews published before the film was televised, producer Kobritz, director Tobe Hooper, and a number of the stars expressed their enthusiasm for the way the project was moving. And indeed there was much to be enthusiastic--even optimistic--about. Working closely with Hooper and Monash, Kobritz introduced a number of changes into the text, designed to emphasize the horror of King's vision and to avoid the palliative effect that innumerable previous treatments of vampires would have had on television audiences.

King's novel, after all, paces itself carefully, building an intolerable tension and malaise before finally revealing the core of evil: the

43

King-vampire Barlow who appears for the first time nearly halfway through the text. In addition, King concentrated more on the fragile and disrupted relationships among people in 'Salem's Lot than upon the vampire; his novel deals more with isolation and distrust as destructive elements than upon the conventional walking undead.

The film, however, would not have the luxury to develop dozens of minor characters--the grotesquely appropriate Mabel Werts and Loretta Starcher; Roy McDougal, trapped in his inability to cope with life; the doomed Dr. Cody; Charlie Rhodes and his schoolbus of vengeful vampires; Dud Rogers and his rat-shooting at the city dump, itself an image for the festering evil at the core of 'Salem's Lot. Even Hubie Marsten would have to be reduced to several lines of dialogue between Ben Mears and Jason Burke over an evening beer.

As a result, several characters coalesced, to the ultimate weakening of the film--a problem King is having with his treatments of The Stand. Cody disappears, merging with Susan Norton's father in the figure of Dr. Bill Norton. Although played capably by Ed Flanders, the character lacks the intensity of Cody, while simultaneously altering the relationship between Mears and Susan Norton.

Another conflation--Corey Bryant with Larry Crockett--allowed Monash to include Bonnie Sawyer's adulterous affair, in keeping with Kobritz's vision of 'Salem's Lot as "Peyton Place turning into vampires" (Kelley, "Salem's Lot" 9), a reference to Kobritz's experiences in the sixties as producer of the television series Peyton Place. While the combination made possible a mildly erotic scene, leading to Crockett (Fred Willard) backing down the steps of the Sawyer home, turning, and coming face to face with the silhouetted hand of the king-vampire, the episode actually retarded rather than impelled the film's movement. King's Corey Bryant was less experienced, an innocent involved with destructive sexuality for the first time--and nearly losing his life, as so many of King's young characters nearly (or actually) lose theirs. The film's Crockett, on the other hand, is a conniver, an older man stereotypically involved with a younger woman. The emphasis has shifted radically, and with it the thematic, imagistic, and imaginative power of the episode. A final combination of Father Callahan with Jason Burke was (wisely) rejected.

In spite of the far-reaching effects these redefinitions of key characters had on the narrative, they represent only a portion of the changes Kobritz introduced, however.

The vampire stands at the center of both the novel and the film. Yet here Kobritz veers most radically from King's text. King's Barlow is verbal, based primarily on Bram Stoker's elegant Count Dracula as visualized by Bela Lugosi in Tod Browning's 1931 film Dracula. King dispenses with the Transylvanian heritage (and presumably with the accent as well), but retains the outlines of the conventional undead.

Kobritz's follows an alternative treatment. In 1922, F. W. Murnau produced an unauthorized adaptation of Stoker's novel, altering the characters' names slightly and retitling the film Nosferatu. Max Schreck's Graf Orlock is tall, gaunt, bald, with deep-set dark-rimmed eyes, elongated claw-like fingers, and protruding incisors rather than the more traditional canines. As Donald F. Glut writes in his The Dracula Book,

> "Schreck's Orlock remains as possibly the most hideous vampire to prowl the screen. His orbs seemed to burn from the blackened eye sockets, which contrasted starkly with the pale face. The ears were pointed, as if belonging to some hellish demon rather than a being that was once a living man . . . . Schreck's Count Orlock was the perfect screen portrayal of a vampire" (cited in Hurwood, Vampires 119).

There is nothing inherently wrong with following the Nosferatu tradition; and Kobritz argued persuasively that the decision to do so stemmed less from an attempt to capitalize on the status of Murnau's film as a horror classic, or on the possibility that Werner Herzog's 1979 re-make would be a commercial success, than on Kobritz's own desire to penetrate to the center of the vampire as horror. "We didn't want a sensual vampire, or one like Lugosi or George Hamilton's," Kobritz said. "We wanted something . . . where the

45

vampire was walking death, ugliness incarnate, a skull that moved and was alive" (Casey 40). Murnau's classic--the "most loathsomely vile vampire to have darkened the door of cinema: bald and stiff as death, with long clutching talons, walking on an undulating carpet of rats" (Lucas Your Movie Guide to Horror 88)--provided the ideal model.

The decision to model Barlow on Orlock might have been justifiable, given Kobritz's vision of the film. Certainly King's brief comment in Danse Macabre (75) indicates no inherent disagreement with the interpretation. The difficulty arises, however, in how the film handles the subsequent vampires. Barlow himself is striking. Withheld from view during most of the film, and in fact appearing directly only three times, he creates a horrifying physical image, particularly for viewers anticipating a suavely elegant Lugosi or Hamilton. The specially created contact lenses that give Barlow's eyes an eerie glow; the wickedly pointed, stained, and rotting incisors; Reggie Nalder's facial angles beneath the make-up; his inarticulate hissing as Barlow rises like a shadow from the Petrie's kitchen floor in his first full scene--all create an effective atmosphere.

The problem is simply that the atmosphere has already been contradicted in the film and will continue to be so.

The horror enveloping 'Salem's Lot uncovers itself slowly in the film--perhaps even more slowly than in the novel. By the time Barlow reveals himself, Ralphie Glick twice appears in vampire form to his brother Danny, and Danny Glick rises from his coffin to infect Mike Ryerson. The first serious mention of vampire occurs almost two hours into the film--and by then, the film has clearly established which tradition it is following. The Glick boys reflect the more traditional Dracula-style vampire: glowing eyes, sallow complexions, and, most critically, elongated canines. Even after Barlow appears, other vampires rise, hiss, and bare their canines: Marjorie Glick in the morgue; Ned Tebbetts and Mike Ryerson in the root cellar of the Marsten House; even Susan Norton in the final scenes of the film.

The decision to fluctuate between the two

traditions leads to interesting questions about the genetics of vampirism. How is it possible for Barlow, representing physically and pschologically Murnau´s Nosferatu, to infect mortals and have them transform into Dracula-types? The problem is not mere quibbling; it underlies one of the basic difficulties in the film. Salem´s Lot overtly attempts to break from the conventions of vampire lore. Mears urges Susan Norton to hang boughs of hawthorne around the house, primarily because Kobritz refused to include any dangerously stereo-typic references to garlic. Similarly, Barlow speaks only one line in the entire film, since Kobritz choices were severely limited:

> I just thought it would be suicidal on
> our part to have a vampire that talks.
> What kind of voice do you put behind a
> vampire? You can´t do Bela Lugosi, or
> you´re going to get a laugh. You can´t
> do Regan in The Exorcist, or you´re go-
> ing to get something that´s unintelligi-
> ble, and besides, you´ve been there
> before. (Kelley "Salem´s Lot" 17).

Kobritz´s solution was twofold: not to allow Barlow to speak until the final scene, with his "Let me go,"; and simultaneously to emphasize the role of Richard Straker (James Mason) as Barlow´s mouthpiece, a decision most obvious in the scene in the Petrie kitchen.

Having gone to such lengths to divorce Barlow from the stereotypic, the conventional, and the already-done, the film subverts its own intentions by peopling ´Salem´s Lot with traditional vampires that pop up from open coffins and rise from morgue slabs. It has been suggested that these second generation vampires represent a larval stage be-tween the draculoid variety and the fully devel-oped Nosferatu; if so, the connection remains un-defined in the film, and that irresolution weakens both the film as a whole and the representation of Barlow in particular.

Another change--this one substantially more successful--centers on the Marsten House itself. Built on a hill overlooking Ferndale, the film location in Northern California (chosen because of its "New England" look), the House is fully as imposing on film as in the novel. From the opening scene, as Ben Mears drives up to the House, it dominates the action. In fact, it grows more dominant as the film progresses, to the point that Kobritz made two key decisions concerning the house.

The first was that the Marsten House should symbolize both Straker and Barlow. Externally imposing, it hides a rotting, polluted interior designed by Mort Rabinowitz. According to Kobritz, Straker is the key to understanding the interior of the House:

> Straker is the human go-between. The shark doesn't choose its own direction, there is a fish that leads it. Straker leads the way; Barlow does the thinking. Straker is his liaison to the world.
> Straker is pristine like the outside of the house. Inside it is a chamber of horrors, representing Straker's inner self. The house is beyond your wildest nightmare; everything rotten, no furniture. Everything falling apart. (Casey 39)

Although the interior shots establish an atmosphere of decay, much of the effect is lost when transferred to a television's small screen. What were originally intended as festering clumps of moss and algae, or as slimy masses erupting from walls and ceilings, fade into an indeterminate background image of ruin. Still, the attempt merits notice; certainly the juxtaposition of the immaculately dapper Straker against the filth of the house emphasizes the opposition between what appears and what is in 'Salem's Lot.

A third change, also centering on the Marsten House, necessitated that the final confrontation between Mears and Barlow be enacted within the house, rather than in the cellar of Eva Miller's boarding house. Dramatically, the decision works. Kobritz's film, supported by Monash's script, reiterates Mear's contention that the house is the center of evil, that the house may itself be evil. In addition, since so much of the last hour of the film takes place in the house, as Susan Norton and Mark Petrie are caught inside it and Mears and

48

Bill Norton arrive to rescue them, it is both con-
venient and logical to continue using the house as
both setting and metaphor.

Again, however, there is a curious disjunc-
ture between what was intended and what happens.
Concentrating on the Marsten House strengthens the
film; suggestions of the Miller Boarding House
from the novel, however, creep in to undercut that
strength. While in the Marsten House, Bill Norton
confronts Straker, who lifts the other man off his
feet (the film does not explain Straker´s super-
human strength; in fact, Mears insists that
Straker is just a man) and impales him against a
wall of antlers. The image is borrowed from
Cody´s death by impalement in the novel; what is
lacking is a coherent rationale for the particular
form. Yet the wall has played no part in the film
to that point; it is almost as if the oddly
mounted antlers were included only to provide an
instrument for Norton´s death. (An interesting
side note: the camera follows Norton´s face in
closeup, allowing his change of expression to
imply his death; in the theatrical version intended for European distribution, Hooper included
a full-body shot of Norton impaled).

A similar influence from the novel appears a
few moments later. Mears and Mark Petrie have
joined to search for Barlow. Mark rushes through
the cellar door and falls--as in the novel, the
stairs have been removed. In the film, though,
the situation dissolves into anti-climax. Rather
than leading to the death of a central character,
the missing stairs occasion only a minor injury:
Mark strains his ankle. The only clear result of
the episode is Mark´s slow response in closing the
root-cellar door on the vampires crawling toward
him as Mears hammers the stake through Barlow´s
heart. Again, the oblique reference to the novel
weakens rather than strengthens the film, even
though Kobritz´s decision to set the climactic
scene in the cellar seems artistically sound.

The end result of all of this care should
have been a memorable film.

It was not.

Ultimately, <u>Salem´s Lot</u> fails as film because
it bores rather than horrifies. In part, this
results from the constraints of television. From
the beginning, the project ran afoul of network

49

standards, including prohibitions against overt violence (an element endemic to vampire films), against showing children threatened (a theme consistent throughout practically everything King has written), against the kind of innovative approach that would have made the film noteworthy against the backdrop of the hundreds of vampire films produced over nearly eight decades.

Other problems stem from production or directorial decisions. The film is unusually slow, particularly for a horror film. Dialogue has been radically cut, again a conscious choice on the part of the production staff. On one hand, this forces an increasingly visual approach to the narrative, appropriate to the film's genre. On the other hand, it results in long passages without dialogue, backed by music that falls and rises to preprogrammed climaxes with numbing regularity.

Midway through the film, Mike Ryerson remains behind after the funeral cortege has left the site of Danny Glick's funeral. He stands at the edge of the grave while the camera shoots from front and back, high-angle and low-angle, and both sides, occasionally cutting to wind tearing at tree branches or knocking down floral wreaths. With a single thirty-second cut to Ben Mears and Jason Burke, the camera remains on Ryerson for a full three minutes as the wind and shifting angles and rising music attempt to create suspense, culminating in Ryerson's jumping onto the coffin and opening it. There is another long moment as the camera focuses on Danny Glick lying against the satin of his casket. Then (no surprise to anyone) the vampire/child rises to press against Ryerson's neck, with a quick fade-out to a commercial. In total, almost five minutes without speech, yet without enough action to hold the viewers' attention.

What dialogue there is tends toward the ponderous and the self-conscious. Blocks of discussion provide background connections to the novel: the history of the Marsten House, Mear's childhood in the Lot (although early in the film, Larry Crockett refers to Mear's remembering a particular street long before it has been established that Mears grew up there). David Soul's interpretation of Ben Mears includes what Soul considered an approach to a literate and intelligent writer (as

opposed to his character on <u>Starsky and Hutch</u>)
(Kelley, "<u>Salem's Lot</u>" 12); yet Mears fluctuates
between slow, almost tongue-tied passages and
near-hysterical claims that the Marsten House is
evil incarnate--a line repeated several times in
the film.

Complicating the difficulties with dialogue
is the simple fact that the film was made for
television--and that includes commercials. The
sense of duration and the rising and falling music
telegraph upcoming breaks; it is no surprise,
then, when the scene freezes and the screen fades
to black just as Danny Glick is about to bite Mike
Ryerson. In other instances, the commercial
breaks simply irritate; Ben Mears and Mark Petrie
are caught in mid-stride as they explore the
Marsten cellar. Following the break, they continue toward the middle of the room, emphasizing
what becomes a frustrating stall in the movement
of the film.

And finally, the conclusion itself raises new
questions. Again departing from the text substantially, Kobritz implies rather than specifies the
burning of 'Salem's Lot--in spite of an overt
reference to a previous fire during Mark Petrie's
school pageant. In the text, a similar reference
had established an imagistic pattern; in the film,
it becomes a throw-away line. Supported by considerations of film-time and expense, Kobritz cuts
from the Marsten House in flames to the final
scene: Ben Mears and Mark Petrie in exile, a re-
prise of the film's opening segment.

In the film's final moments, Mears comes face
to face with Susan Norton, seductively dressed,
artfully arranged on a bed. For a moment, he
falls under her spell--then her eyes open, glowing
at him. In a moment viewers have been waiting for
since she appeared on the screen, she opens her
mouth, reveals her true nature. As with the
bloody hand in <u>Carrie</u>, or the werewolf's final
gasp in <u>Silver Bullet</u>, the scene startles without
horrifying, leaving viewers uncomfortable and dis-
satisfied. After all, the glowing holy water let
us know long moments before that there was a
vampire nearby. In its conclusion, then, as in so
many other elements, <u>Salem's Lot</u> falls back on the
stereotypes it once attempted to avoid.

Casting generally works. Lance Kerwin is an

effective and convincing Mark Petrie, resembling Soul physically but more controlled throughout. James Mason handles his expanded role as Straker with wit, even managing to make some rather un- likely lines sound almost natural--particularly his lines to Father Callahan during the confronta- tion in the Petries´ kitchen. Other characters lend strength to the film: Ed Flanders´s Bill Norton; Bonnie Bedelia´s Susan Norton. Marie Windsor and Elisha Cook work effectively together, some twenty-three years after their roles in <u>The Killing</u>. Reggie Nalder is ideal as Barlow, true to Murnau´s original vision, with the enhancements of such contemporary special effects as contact lenses and hand-crafted teeth. David Soul comes across as a frenetic man; a writer who types with one-finger, deeply convinced that a house can be evil but oddly resistant to the possibility of vampires. By the end of the film, he loses touch even with the realities he imagined he once knew.

His performance sums up the difficulties of the film. It tries for new interpretations but ultimately falls back on the old. Barlow crushes Father Callahan´s crucifix, suggesting the the old tales about vampires and crosses are invalid; yet Ben Mears´s impromptu tongue-depressor cross burns into Marjorie Glick´s forehead and discorporates her. It is all right for the film to break with the tradition; it is difficult for it to break with and simultaneously try to uphold the conven- tions.

More than anything, <u>Salem´s Lot</u> indicates the difficulty of translating Stephen King´s works to television. The words are frequently there; the characters (or facsimiles of them) are present; the narrative line continues largely undisturbed. But Stephen King is missing. The interest he gen- erates, the sense of realism that underlies his every narrative, and the concentration on the readers´ reality have disappeared. In this case, it is easily to stipulate a cause: the sanitizing effect of commercial television. In spite of the care expended on it, in spite of the time allowed to present the story, in spite of the special ef- fects, <u>Salem´s Lot</u> fails to rise above the crowd. It remains one of many vampire films, no less in- teresting than most, but no more exciting, either.

CHAPTER V

The Shining (1980)

King's The Shining remains among his most
teachable novels; in an informal discussion at the
International Conference on the Fantastic in the
Arts (1984), King in fact noted that when his
works find their ways into college or university
literature courses, The Shining is the most likely
to appear.

Several points account for the novel's popularity as a classroom text. It is consciously
(and often self-consciously) literary in its allu-
siveness, with references ranging from Shakespeare
and Dr. Johnson to Arthur Miller and Truman Ca-
pote, with frequent stops along the way for brief
nods to Emily Dickinson, T. S. Eliot, William Carlos Williams, Peter Straub, and a host of other
literary luminaries, including Edgar Allan Poe.
It becomes in some senses a compendium of the
literature which has preceded it, summarizing and
transforming multiple themes, techniques, and
devices as it moves through its own narrative of
hauntings and madness.

In addition, the novel is equally consciously an artifact concerned with the creation of art-
ifacts--a metafiction of sorts. Jack Torrance
stands not only at the center of King's narrative
but at the creative center of his own literary
work, his play-in-progress. The relationships between Torrance's life and his attitudes toward
literature become an important motif in The Shining, until life and art finally merge as Jack
creates his own imagined realities.

And finally, The Shining is unique among
King's fictions for the strong thread of conscious
symbol-making that functions as a corollary to
Torrance's literary pretensions. Throughout, Torrance translates his experiences into symbolic
statements, most obviously when he encounters the
wasps while repairing the Overlook roof. For
pages at a time, Torrance indulges in symbol
making, explaining his life, with the wasps, the

53

roof, and the Overlook itself as metaphors.   From
this perspective, The Shining is an ideal vehicle
in itself to introduce and discuss the literary
dimensions of contemporary dark fantasy.
     Perhaps these inherent qualities in the novel
stimulated Stanley Kubrick´s initial interest in
filming The Shining; at the least, they contribute
to the unique texture of the completed film, since
Kubrick attempted to translate into film many of
the literary charactersitics of King´s novel. The
result is, as one might expect, certainly the most
controversial film version of any King work to
date; only The Stand and Pet Sematary, both now in
production, might lead to more difficulties in
representation than did The Shining.
     Initially, of course, the coupling of King
and Kubrick seemed ideal--the most popular writer
of horror fiction and the most prestigious director in science-fiction and fantasy films. Many
looked to Kubrick´s work on the novel to become a
crucial statement (if not the definitive statement) on the nature of horror film. Dan Christen-
sen´s "Stephen King: Living in ´Constant, Deadly
Terror´" noted that none of the projects relating
to filming King´s work was as "promising, or as
intriguing" as what Kubrick was doing with The
Shining (30). David Schow´s "Return of the Curse
of the Son of Mr. King: Book Two" went even further. The clear failure of Salem´s Lot to do
justice to King on the television screen

          brought audiences, with trembling antici-
          pation, into theatres to catch The Shin-
          ing, whose attendant production mythology
          was enough to suggest a classic film at
          the very least; at most a milestone in
          cinematic horror, or something to justify
          the reactionary plaudits given the film
          by critics who, though zealous, were con-
          spicuously few in number. (51)

     Even after production, King remained publicly
enthusiastic about the film. In "Horrors," an article in TV Guide identifying the ten scariest
films on videocassettes and discs, King listed The
Shining as his fifth choice, commenting that while
the film diverges greatly from his novel, it nonetheless "builds a claustrophobic terror in a re-

54

lentless way" into the narrative. "Could it have been done better?" he asks, then reponds: "Over the years I've come to believe that it probably could not. The film is cold and disappointingly loveless--but chilling" (56).

Originally, Kubrick apparently intended to follow King's plot closely, although rumors circulated for some time that the film would probably diverge widely from King's text; in fact, when Christensen questioned King about the persistent rumors, King said that he had

> asked Stanley how close he was following the plot and he said extremely closely. There are going to be some minor changes, but nothing substantial. In terms of plot, it's going to follow the book very closely; whether or not it's going to follow the book in spirit is something else again." ("Living" 31-32)

In terms of Kubrick's diverging from the original text, however, in an interview published in 1978, Peter S. Perakos elicited the following comment from King:

> From the beginning, when I first talked to Kubrick some months ago, he wanted to change the ending. He asked me for my opinion on Halloran [sic] becoming possessed, and then finishing the job that Torrance started, killing Danny, Wendy, and lastly himself. Then, the scene would shift to the spring, with a new caretaker and his family arriving. However, the audience would see Jack, Wendy, and Danny in an idyllic family scene--as ghosts--sitting together, laughing and talking. And I saw a parallel between this peaceful setting at the end of the picture and the end of 2001 where the astronaut is transported to the Louis XIV bedroom. To me, the two endings seemed to tie together. ("On Carrie" 14)

After discussions with Kubrick, King apparently (and accurately) believed that Kubrick had aban-

doned that highly unlikely conclusion; such an
overly optimistic treatment of the idea that spir-
it continues beyond life would contradict too
strongly what had gone on before in the film. Ku-
brick´s conclusion avoided that difficulty, while
raising a number of others.

If King had any immediate reservations about
the project at that, they apparent lay more with
casting than with the screenplay. King´s Wendy
Torrance is strong, beautiful, and intelligent;
Shelley Duvall, he noted, "just looks sort of nervous and overbred." Jack Torrance, on the other
hand, was not "the Jack Nicholson type at all; not
flamboyant, almost withdrawn. I had someone like
Martin Sheen in mind. But nobody will talk about
that sort of thing in preproduction. What they
want to talk about is someone who´s bankable--and
Nicholson is that" (Christensen, "Living" 32).

Certain elements of initial production led to
odd parallels between King and Kubrick. One of
the most daring divergences in the film is Ku-
brick´s use of a hedge maze rather than a topiary
garden--and a subsequent re-writing of major portions of the narrative. In an interview, King
noted that it was

> very funny to me that he chose a hedge
> maze, because my original concept <u>was</u> to
> create a hedge maze. And the reason
> that I rejected the idea in favor of the
> topiary animals was because of an old
> Richard Carlson film, THE MAZE. The
> story was about a maze, of course, but
> in the middle of the maze was a pond.
> And in the middle of the pond, on a lily
> pad, was <u>grandfather</u> who was a <u>frog</u>.
> Every night, grandpa turned into a frog
> and so they had to put him into the
> pond. To me, that was <u>ludicrous</u>. So I
> abandoned the idea of a hedge. (Perakos,
> "On <u>Carrie</u>" 14)

Kubrick´s decision to replace the topiary animals
with a hedge maze seems appropriate in the context
of the film as completed. The maze as image is
central to Kubrick--witness the subtitle of Thomas
Allen Nelson´s full-length of Kubrick´s films,
"Inside a Film Artist´s Maze," as well as mazes

and puzzles in films such as 2001 and A Clockwork Orange. In addition, trying to animate hedge animals might have led to the added difficulty of creatures that resembled Disney characters.

In her review of the film prior to its release as a network film, Judith Crist noted that it "provides us with the ultimate in horror." Although she is aware of the changes Kubrick introduced into the structure of the narrative--particularly Kubrick's emphasis on family relationships rather than setting--Crist states that

> As the sense of menace unreels in the brightly lit and handsomely furbished public rooms, in the mysteries behind a locked door, the echoing footfalls and the flashes of horrifying hallucination, the child becomes our medium, the father our menace. The film's triumph is Nicholson's in his minutely portrayed transition from ordinary householder to Mephistophelean madman: his is the true tool of terror. (A5-A6)

Thus far, we have been concentrating on the film as a reflection (however varied or skewed) of Stephen King. More than any other of the films based on King's fictions, however, The Shining requires more. Kubrick is, after all, responsible for several of the most successful--and most controversial--films of the past three decades. From the beginning of his career, Kubrick attempted to incorporate his personal vision into every film he made; and, with few exceptions, he succeeded in this attempt. His earliest films were experimental or documentary shorts: Day of the Fight (1951); Flying Padre (1951); The Seafarers (1953). In 1953 he produced, directed, photographed, and edited Fear and Desire; two years later, he co-produced, directed, photographed, edited, and scripted Killer's Kiss. The next two films, The Killing (1956) and Paths of Glory (1957), were products of Harris-Kubrick Productions, with Kubrick directing and participating in writing the screenplay.

With Spartacus (1960), Kubrick's role was radically limited. Stepping in to replace director Anthony Mann, Kubrick was restricted from many of the freedoms he had enjoyed; he found himself instead in the position of a typical Hollywood studio director: responsible for directing the actors, composing shots, and supervising editing. "What is missing from the list," Nelson points out, "is that script control which was crucial to the artistry of The Killing and Paths of Glory, and which has lent distinction to all his films since Paths with the lone exception of Spartacus (Kubrick 55). The result was less Kubrick-on-film than Kirk Douglas and Dalton Trumbo.

Following Spartacus, Kubrick re-asserted his particular vision on his films by retaining greater control over the finished products. He directed Lolita (1962); and co-produced, directed, and partially scripted Dr. Strangelove, or How I Learned to Stop Worrying and Love the Bomb (1964). With 2001: A Space Odyssey (1968), Kubrick's hand became even more apparent. He produced and directed the film, working with Arthur C. Clarke in writing the screenplay (as an interesting sidelight, Clarke frequently watched the day's rushes before writing portions of the novel; in a sense, novel and film were produced simultaneously, a daring oddity in this day of novelizations from commercially successful films). In addition, Kubrick received screen-credits for designing and directing special photographic effects; and, given the increasingly complex and sophisticated integration of classical music into the backgrounds of Kubrick's subsequent films, it must be assumed that he played a major role in selecting the music as well--by Richard Strauss, Johann Strauss, Aram Khachaturian, and Gyorgy Ligeti.

In one of Kubrick's most powerful, impressive, and artistically designed films, A Clockwork Orange (1971), Kubrick again retained control by producing, directing, writing the screenplay from Anthony Burgess's novel, and setting the visual image to music from Beethoven, Edward Elgar, Rossini, Purcell, Rimsky-Korsakov, and others.

Kubrick's 1975 version of Barry Lyndon, while not a commercial success, continued his exploration of a specific vision. He again acted as producer, director, and screenplay writer, with John Alcott in charge of photography for a second time (the first time in Clockwork)--he would also direct photography for Kubrick's next film, The

Shining. Music, as before, was drawn from a variety of sources: Bach, Frederick the Great, Handel, Mozart, Schubert, Vivaldi.

By the time we arrive at The Shining, then, several patterns have become apparent in Kubrick's work, most critically his determination to retain control of a film's final form. By doing so, he was able to stamp the text--whether original or based on important novels--with his own particular trademark. His choice of John Alcott for a third film suggests that he found Alcott's work especially appropriate in expressing visually what Kubrick saw as the underlying conceptions of a film. And the background music for The Shining, while not as intrusively present or inextricably connected with the narrative as was Beethoven to A Clockwork Orange, nonetheless furthers Kubrick's explorations: the eerie sounds of Bartok, Ligeti, Krzystof Penderecki, Wendy Carlos and Rachel Elkin develop almost an independent existence within the context of the film.

It is not surprising then (or rather, should not have been surprising, since many viewers of the film claimed surprise) that The Shining should turn out to be as much Stanley Kubrick as Stephen King, if not moreso. Nor is it surprising that viewers expecting Stephen King should react angrily, often venomously, when given a different "SK": Stanley Kubrick. Schow's vigorous conclusion is simply that Kubrick proved himself incapable of handling King's material: "And if The Shining is really that American Gothic portrait of the death of a family relationship, just what is Kubrick--an American expatriate--doing filming it?" The film is, in a word, "boring." (54-55).

Nevertheless, the film and its director-producer-screenwriter are not without their supporters. F. Anthony Macklin begins his "Understanding Kubrick: The Shining" by acknowledging that most viewers dislike the film. There are, however, good reasons for that dislike--and, he contends, for ultimately appreciating the film, in spite of the fact that it diverged from King's text and that it did not use conventional treatments to create terror or horror. Instead, one must approach the film from a different perspective, namely, that the film represents not King, not horror as a genre, but the unique vision of Stan-

59

ley Kubrick. To do so brings five main points in focus.

First, the characters in the film seem flat and banal because Kubrick <u>wants</u> them to; the texture of the film is in fact carefully built up, resulting not from miscasting but from Kubrick´s underlying philosophy. In this sense, the film should be compared to Kubrick´s own <u>2001</u> instead of to King´s novel. The interview with Ullman, Macklin points out, owes more to the intentionally uncommunicative briefing scene in <u>2001</u> than to King´s crisp, precise dialogue.

Second, Kubrick´s films continually explore outlets for aggression--most specifically the apes in <u>2001</u>, Alex in <u>A Clockwork Orange</u>, and certainly Jack Torrance in <u>The Shining</u>. Jack´s aimless wanderings in the Overlook--his pointless one-man games of catch, his obsessive typing of a single line--indicate his lack of outlet. The point is underscored, Macklin notes, by Kubrick´s recurrent use of Roadrunner cartoons as background. Danny watches one at the beginning of the film; Larry Durkin´s television shows one when Hallorann arrives to rent a snowcat; and Danny is again watching one when Wendy goes downstairs and sees Jack´s manuscript. The explicit violence in the relationship between the Roadrunner and Wile E. Coyote has specific analogues throughout the film.

Third, for Kubrick, objects and machines are almost more important than people. Certainly in <u>Dr. Strangelove</u> and <u>2001</u> that sense emerges; in <u>The Shining</u>, Kubrick focuses on the maze, for example, as an external object that reveals the inner natures of Jack, Wendy, and Danny.

Fourth, the problems most viewers had with characterization in the film are in fact responses to Kubrick´s intentions. Nicholson has been accused of "everything from being boring to overacting" (94), Macklin notes. More accurately, however, Nicholson is responding to a difficult task. He must blend the banality and absurdity of Kubrick´s view of the character, constantly destroying his own chances to rise above either. Consequently, he "changes from the banal would-be writer in the interview to the absurd, impulsive extrovert at the bar to the lively, vicious killer at the end" (94). To do so requires that he <u>not</u> give a coherent, polished performance--and viewers disparage him for not doing so.

And fifth, Kubrick´s The Shining is satirical in ways that King´s novel is not. Kubrick sees American culture as "a cartoon and a caricature," Macklin concludes, intruding parodies of Nixon and Johnny Carson at seemingly inappropriate moments. Even the concluding photograph implicitly critiques contemporary American society by juxtaposing it with an image of 1921, post-war, celebratory America--one which no longer exists.

Given these five points, Macklin argues, viewers are almost bound to misinterpret Kubrick´s intentions. The film is complex, but repays careful attention. Visual techniques impel interest; and, "with the added awareness that banality, aggression, objects, ordinary characters, and satire often play a meaningful part in a Kubrick film, we should be able to deal with it" (95).

Approaching Kubrick from another perspective, Greg Keeler refers briefly to King´s article in the January, 1981 issue of Playboy, citing the comment that horror films are like "lifting a trap door in the civilized forebrain and throwing a basket of raw meat to the hungry alligators swimming around in the subterranean river beneath." He then compares several mainstream films about the disintegration of the family--Ordinary People, Tribute, Kramer vs. Kramer--to such films as Burnt Offerings, The Amityville Horror, and The Shining. "Though they all ostensibly deal with uppity houses," he says, they "are also about families going to pieces. They are gatorland´s answer to the touching melodramas of the forebrain" (2).

Point by point, Keller analyzes Kramer vs. Kramer, identifying theme, plot, characterization, language, and episode. For each, he finds horrific analogues in The Shining, a dark counterpoint focusing on the nightmare rather than the melodrama. The comparisons lead to the conclusion that "no matter how one views the differences between these films, there is no doubt that the family has to disintegrate for the characters to survive, either physically or psychologically" (8).

Yet another approach to The Shining concentrates on its place in Kubrick´s oeuvre. Nelson´s "Remembrance of Things Forgotten: The Shining" forms the final chapter in Kubrick: Inside a Film Artist´s Maze. As such, it suggests ways in which

61

the film culminates much that had gone on before in Kubrick´s work. Nelson carefully details themes, images, cinematic details of set, characterization, casting, and editing--all pointing to Kubrick´s control over the final film. Additionally, Nelson casts back to suggest references throughout The Shining to Kubrick´s earlier films, including a half-facetious discussion of the number 21 in interpreting Kubrick´s maze/puzzle images. "Numerically speaking," he concludes, "The Shining is 2001 in reverse gear" (230).

All of this is to argue that perhaps the best approach to Kubrick´s The Shining is to divorce it from connections with Stephen King--not because Kubrick failed to do justice to King´s narrative, but simply because it has ceased to be King´s. While the film´s opening panorama effectively sets the mood for both the novel and the film, the first shots of the Torrances suggest how radically Kubrick has in fact departed from King´s original. Casting does create serious problems if one insists upon King´s Torrances; yet Kubrick´s Wendy is appropriately dissociated from romantic love. There is nothing in Duvall´s performance to suggest the relationship between King´s Wendy and Jack. Instead, she clearly represents an exclusively maternal figure, standing between husband and son as protector for the latter, antagonist to the former. For her to do so alienates the viewer expecting King´s Wendy; her stance is, however, critical to Kubrick´s.

Similarly, Nicholson´s performance remains ambivalent. He is not King´s Jack Torrance. King makes it clear that the evil in his novel is centered in the Overlook itself. The manta-shaped shadow that escapes from the shattered window of the Presidential Suite is an external evil that has dominated the hotel; once it escapes, the Overlook becomes merely an empty hull, justifiably destroyed in cleansing flames. Evil has not been defeated, merely displaced; in fact, not until IT (1986) will King allow a clear and permanent defeat of an evil force.

This sense disappears in Kubrick´s film. Nicholson´s Jack Torrance in large part replaces the Overlook as focus of evil. From the opening scenes, he is clearly dissociated from his family--and from himself. There is no emotional con-

62

nection between him Wendy or Danny. His progress in the film details increasing fragmentation and degeneration. Yet in an important way, he stands at the center of the tragedy, displacing Danny in crucial scenes. The film Danny escapes, not through Hallorann's aid as in the novel, but by luring his own father into the frozen maze and abandoning him--effectively killing his father and rescuing his mother in what may be an oddly Oedipal image. And, since the film Jack has also largely supplanted the Overlook as well, there is no need to destroy the structure; given Kubrick's re-interpretation of the narrative, to do so would be to resort to stereotypic pyrotechnic special effects for a climax. Instead, he literally focuses on Jack Torrance, on the photograph in the empty hotel.

Again and again, Kubrick replaces critical points in the novel, constructing his own narrative that touches only tangentially on King's. The wasps disappear, and along with them Jack's opportunity for conscious image-making; Kubrick's Jack is incapable of such depth of perception. For him, the replacement image of the maze is doubly appropriate--visually as Jack loses himself in the maze-like corridors of the hotel (which he never leaves until the final scene; leaving it means death for Jack), and psychologically in the mazes of his own madness. The roque mallet also disappears, replaced by the more overtly violent axe, which in turn juxtaposes nicely with Nicholson's insane "Heeerre's Johnny" parody as he breaks into the apartment. Even the animated fire hose--which King notes actually formed the initial image for writing the novel ("On The Shining" 16)--disappears.

In exchange, Kubrick adds his own imagistic complexity to the film. Mazes appear and recur . . . in the carpeting, in the intricate angles of corridors and rooms, in the model inside the hotel, in the actual maze outside. In an interesting cut-shot, Jack in fact stares down at the model; as the camera drawn nearer and nearer, the viewer discovers Wendy and Danny walking at the center of the maze, and Kubrick has neatly bridged inner and outer, Jack's inability to solve mazes with Wendy and Danny's need for experience outside the hotel.

Similarly, Danny's incessant riding through corridors on his big-wheel not only touches on the maze image but reflects back to Kubrick's treatment of sound and silence in <u>2001</u>. As the big-wheel crosses from wooden floor to carpet (usually with an intricate maze-like pattern), the abrasive sound ceases, creating an irregular regularity in sound and silence reminiscent of the astronauts' breathing in the earlier film. And, also reminiscent of <u>2001</u>, Kubrick consistently frames shots through stark, angular, geometrically precise openings, with organic movement and shape caught within unmoving, artificial regularity.

Throughout the film, at every level from script to casting to set design, Kubrick imbues <u>The Shining</u> with his own personality, his own vision. And his images work. They are not King's, but they <u>do</u> work. To that extent, Kubrick film <u>does</u> resemble King's novel. Both are eminently "teachable," self-consciously literary/artistic manifestations of theme, imagery, symbolism. Both demonstrate creative talents focused on a single narrative, exploring the possibilities of verbal and visual representation, of novel into film.

CHAPTER VI

Creepshow (1982)

As a film, Creepshow represented a change of pace from the productions that preceded it. Among other things, it provided several first opportunities for both King and George A. Romero.

* It was Romero's first crack at a big-budget film, $8 million , almost twenty times the budget for his classic Night of the Living Dead. It also allowed him to work with established stars of the caliber of E. G. Marshall . . . in a horror film.

* It was King's first creative and financial involvement in filming one of his novels. He wrote the screenplay as well, and acted in the film.

* It was their first collaborative effort, a precursor, as it were, to The Stand and Pet Sematary. It virtually became a test-case, to determine whether King and Romero would be able to find backing for the later, more ambitious projects.

The film also attempted several difficult tasks, not the least of which was to recreate successfully on film the tone and texture of the E. C. comics which had so strongly influenced both King and Romero. In addition, it attempted to do so by using an anthology format, a form that had already proven unsuccessful for several other films. And, it would include several original pieces by King, rather than adaptations of already completed works.

Taking all of this into consideration, it became obvious that Creepshow did indeed represent a shift in direction in King films, moving away from the psychological impact of Carrie, the conventionality of Salem's Lot, and the idiosyncratic, private vision of Kubrick's The Shining. For the first time, horror would be paramount. King's express purpose in doing the film was to create a film to counter the innumerable "ripoffs" of Carpenter's Halloween then appearing. Certainly the opening shots of Creepshow, with the full-front view of a white clap-board house complete with Jack-o-lantern in the front window, were designed to make reflexive connections with Carpenter's film.

On the other hand, King also intended that Creepshow as much undercut the genre as emphasize it. While he noted that he and Romero hoped to create a film that would "scare people so continuously that they'd have to crawl out of the theater," he also said that while writing the script (in sixty days, ending in October 1979), his idea was "that the audience would be screaming and laughing at the same time" (Gagne, "Creepshow" 20).

Horror and laughter--the dual keys to Creepshow. The broad comedy of "The Lonesome Death of Jordy Verrill," largely created by King's portrayal of the title character but also emphasized by the narrative itself, epitomizes humor; the tightly paced suspense and overt violence of "The Crate" or the inexorable and incremental presence of roaches (over 20,000 of them) in "They're Creeping Up on You" provides the horror.

As far as critics were concerned, however, the primary question was whether Creepshow generated as much horror or terror as it did simple disgust through what King has called the "gross-out." Michael Sragow's review in Rolling Stones finds for the latter:

> The new, five-part anthology-movie Creepshow, written by King and directed by George Romero . . . is a salute to the cult-beloved EC horror comic books of the early Fifties. As a movie Creepshow is negligible, but as a cultural indicator, it's terrific--a big clue to what even the most skillful and likable schlock-horror purveyors have been up to in all those years since 1957's I Was a Teenage Werewolf. They want to make an

66

enormous catharsis for hundreds of thousands of slobs and to make slobs out of
nonslobs. To them, the lowest common
denominator isn´t a term of derision but
an admirable goal." (48)

Sragow refers to King´s comments in Danse Macabre
about the nature of horror and terror--on the
physical, visceral, neurological component of horror as opposed to the more intellectual perception
in terror that unknown forces are arrayed against
characters. Beneath both, however, lies simple
revulsion--the "gag reflex"--with its overtly man-
ipulative base in visual representations of the
"gross out." What concerns Sragow most about
Creepshow is that King and Romero consistently
work toward that third level, especially in "Fa-
ther´s Day," "The Crate," and "They´re Creeping Up
on You." The five episodes of the film contain,
by actual count, "three walking corpses, one sui-
cidal living weed, a Tasmanian devil who sinks her
teeth into three victims, a few vivid deaths by
drowning . . . and one death by cockroaches." Humor and horror are too broadly detailed, depending
upon parodies of film and television cliches (48).
    King sees the situation from quite a dif-
ferent light, of course. For him, "E. C. Comics
were the last gasp of romanticism in America. The
scales were always put back in balance, even if
that meant this decomposing, rotting corpse had to
get out of the ground and go after the people who
killed him" (Gagne, "Creepshow" 21). King´s comment recognizes tacitly the essence of Sragow´s
criticism. At the same time, however, it suggests
another level of interpretation, or at least of
interest. Seen in this light, the E. C. Comics
--and Creepshow, in its re-creation of them--be-
come as much contemporary morality plays as anything else, in which, as Bob Martin says, "the
wicked, the greedy, the conspiratorial are brought
to an unmerciful end, usually through the inter-
vention of an anonymous supernatural force--fate"
("On [and Off] the Set" 43).
    This element is important in understanding
much of what happens in Creepshow. Much like their
medieval predecessors, the episodes of Creepshow
depend upon broadly delineated characters and situations. There are few nuances of interpretation:

67

good characters are good and bad characters are truly evil. Hal Holbrook's Harry Northrup is unbelievably patient and long-suffering at the hands of his harridan-shrew wife, Adrienne Barbeau's Wilma (Billie) Northrup. King's Jordy Verrill is innocently naive to the point of absurdity--a critical element in his episode. Upson Pratt's villainy surpasses everything published in the National Inquirer and other such publications about the secret lives of the rich and powerful.

In each case, characters are over-drawn, the stereotypes extended to impossible lengths, the conflicts between them reduced to simplistic good and evil. True, Ted Danson's Harry Wentworth and Gaylen Ross's Becky Vickers are presumably guilty of adultery; that crime, however, does not justify the revenge taken by Leslie Nielson as Richard Vickers. The outright cruelty of Richard Vickers' chosen mode of exacting that revenge--and his obvious delight in watching his victims' suffering--does justify their subsequent revenge as they come from their watery graves to exact retribution.

The world of Creepshow is an inordinately moral place, resembling in part the universe one encounters in such tales as Poe's "The Black Cat," in which evil actions bring about certain and immediate retribution. The one episode in Creepshow which seems not to delineate such a world is, in fact, "The Lonesome Death of Jordy Verrill." Originally published as "Weeds," the narrative was intended as the opening chapter of a novel King began shortly after completing Carrie. Upon finishing the episode, with the green invasion moving inexorably toward town, King discovered that he "couldn't find any more to say" (Gagne, Creepshow 21). To that degree, the tale represents a different narrative thrust from the other four in Creepshow; it deals with an individual, isolated by physical space and by psychological distance from the rest of humankind. There are no evil actions, and consequently no immediate retribution. And, although the episode is certainly the most comic of the five, it is in some ways the most unsettling. Were Verrill less one-dimensional, less absurd, less childish in his actions and reactions, the horror of his death would surmount anything else in the film. As it is, King's portrayal defuses the horror, allowing viewers (perhaps forcing them) to laugh instead of cry.

In the other episodes, however, the sense of retribution builds as the narratives progress, culminating in the roach-death of Upson Pratt, destroyed by that which he fears the most and by that which best defines himself in relation to the rest of humankind. Or, perhaps better said, the film actually culminates with the voodoo torture of an unfeeling father, completing the opening frame-narrative of the film.

Given this morality-play background, several other decisions make better sense. Characters are continually removed from settings; in "Father's Day," for example, the flashbacks detailing Nathan Grantham's cruelty and his ultimate death are literally framed on the screen, becoming cinematic analogues to comic-book frames. At the same time, the framing sets characters and their actions apart from the more realistic settings seen during the rest of the episodes. Their isolation is complete; we see their evil, both inherent and actual, without any distractions. Similarly, at moments of extreme terror--usually associated with the instant revenge is exacted--backdrops disappear, replaced by back-lit scrim that reproduces the flat, violently colored backgrounds of comic-book frames--brilliant reds, yellows, white, and black. Again, the simplicity and startling vividness of background heightens the sense of justice restored . . . or at least vengeance completed. (The backdrop colors are in fact so intense that the film developers complained that Romero's camera crews had overexposed portions of the film).

On a narrative level, the morality-play tradition requires a streamlining of episodes. Nothing is included that does not lead directly to the predetermined statement; there are no subplots, few extraneous characters, little attempt to develop psychological complexity. Again as in many of their medieval counterparts, these episodes have a single purpose--to illustrate the workings of a supernatural force in exacting retribution. Everything is subsumed to that straight-line development. As a result, with few exceptions, characters do not change. Jordy Verrill remains absurdly naive throughout; Upson

Pratt merely reveals increasing depths of callous-
ness and egocentricity.

On the other hand, King was aware of an inherent difficulty in re-creating this faithfully
the skewed world-view of E. C. Comics to a generation of viewers three decades removed from the
original readers. To the question, "How can one
present such a world-view in the 1980´s without
sounding corny," King answered:

> One thing you can´t do is come down on
> that as a conscious part of every epi-
> sode. It´s simply there. It´s waiting
> for people to pick it up, and you hope,
> when they do, that it still works. But
> the movie doesn´t at all depend on peo-
> ple picking up the E. C. elements,
> though I hope they do. I´m kind of ex-
> pecting they will, because whenever I
> mention them, everybody nods, and seems
> to have very fond memories of what those
> comics were like. (Martin, "On [and Off]
> the Set" 43)

As with the earlier films, however, there is
more to Creepshow than simply this one critical
approach. It, too, represents the unique vision
of others besides Stephen King.

The influence of George A. Romero is, of
course, important in the film, just as Stanley Kubrick stands behind The Shining. The difference
here lies in King´s involvement in the project,
re-writing scenes as situations required, constantly expressing himself in the text.

The individual episodes of Creepshow differ
greatly in tone and effect, yet all contribute to
the overall sense of justice and retribution. From
the opening shots, Romero uses odd camera angles,
carefully orchestrated comic-book effects, and the
implied violence of the father´s language (as well
as King´s trademark parent-versus-child treatment)
to suggest the kinds of episodes to come.

The first, "Father´s Day," is in some ways
the most overtly related to the E. C. tradition.
The traditional elements of horror are present: a
hideous crime perpetrated in the past and as yet
unrevenged; a family held together by the horrible
secret . . . and by greed; an idiosyncratic char-

70

acter who acts as stimulus for the horror; settings designed to emphasize horrific possibilities. At the same time, small touches paradoxically increase and lighten the sense of terror. Harry Blaine constantly strikes matches at inopportune moments--the first time, he is handed the murder-weapon ashtray; the last time, he strikes it on a stone cherub in the cemetery, giving his fate a curious sense of appropriateness. In perhaps the most visual image in the episode, a bloody, decaying hand bursts through the soil at the foot of Grantham's tombstone; given the controversial nature of De Palma's ending for Carrie and the reflexive nature of Creepshow, it seems likely that King and Romero intended not only to shock viewers with an E. C. motif, but to remind those same viewers of their reactions to Carrie.

Elsewhere in the story, characters find that justice can be more than cruel. Aunt Bedelia finally lies with a young man . . . as Harry Blaine falls next to her in the open grave, then is joined with her (literally) as the heavy tombstone falls on them both. The accompanying sound effects are both understated and highly effective--a muted squish. From that point, Nathan Grantham's corpse systematically destroys the household, culminating with the Carrie Nye-birthday cake.

"The Lonesome Death of Jordy Verrill" is the least horrific, yet potentially the most touching. There are no "creatures," except for a rather Lovecraftian meteorite; it alters Verrill's farm in ways opposite to those of Lovecraft's The Colour Out of Space. Instead of turning everything a brittle, dusty, unearthly gray and ultimately consuming Nahum Gardner and his family, as in Lovecraft's story, this meteor brings about an effloresence of greenery, not limited to the soil. For the most part, King and Romero work for broad comedy: Jordy Verrill's distorted visions of the university professor and the doctor; his carefully limited dialogue, suggesting an equally limited intellectual range; and the ironic counterpart of the television programs in the background, concluding with the promise that Castle County will green up faster than anyone can imagine.

The episode does indeed seem designed for fun. We see Stephen King giving a creditable performance in his own script. We watch the inexorable progress of the eerie green stuff--but without any deep sense of threat. Only at the end, when Verrill is completely covered with growth and his voice is distorted almost beyond recognition (and King did not wear the final costume) does the episode seek for horror.

In a sense, however, this episode demonstrates most clearly the sub-themes developed in Creepshow. The alien growth seems almost designed more as metaphor than as horrific element. The episode ignores for the moment the quasi-cosmic vengeance assumed in the others and concentrates on one of the most important themes in horror: isolation. Verrill is already isolated physically, mentally, and emotionally. His single vision of his father (significantly played by the same actor as portrayed the threatening professor and the equally threatening doctor) provides no comfort, and Verrill consciously chooses to ignore the visionary father's advice. Ignoring it brings death, but there is no evidence that following it would have had any different result. Again and again, Romero demonstrates Verrill's isolation and separation; to that extent, the alien growth is only a visible manifestation of something that had already doomed Verrill. His death becomes more the acknowledgement of the inevitable than a horrific vengeance for some earlier hideous crime. "The Lonesome Death of Jordy Verrill" thus seems closer in feeling and tone to King's fictions than do the other episodes; here, momentarily, King has allowed himself to be diverted from the E. C. re-creations into something approaching a thematic treatment.

Not so "Something to Tide You Over." The episode strongly parallels King's "The Ledge," first a short story and later a segment in Cat's Eye. Although King has said that the parallels did not occur to him until after Creepshow was completed, "Something to Tide You Over" seems almost designed as a counter-piece to the earlier story. In "The Ledge" there is no supernatural horror; everything, however hideous or horrific, is drawn from our world. The most memorable moments--the pigeon pecking at Stan Norris's ankles, for example--are fully explainable within the universe we know and understand. And the

72

story concludes in the middle of the action; Cressner has not yet returned, and if he should somehow survive the ledge, it seems clear that Norris will "welch" on the bet. Either way, Cressner is doomed, although the reader never discovers how precisely how.

In "Something to Tide You Over," King shifts protocols. The supernatural plays a large part in the narrative, although the remaining elements nicely follow. The betrayed husbands--Cressner and Richard Vickers--both set themselves above law and acceptable morality, obsessive in their desires to possess. The protagonists--Norris and Wentworth--are younger, impulsive, naively unaware of their opponents' acquisitiveness. The women filling out the triangle, Marcia Cressner and Becky Vickers, remain ciphers. Both are doubly sacrificed, once to their younger lovers' inability to judge situations, and again to their respective husbands' insane possessiveness. Neither plays a functional role in the narrative; in the film versions, they are barely on screen at all, as the cameras concentrate on the antagonism between husbands and lovers.

The episode in fact fragments into two distinct "horror" tales. The first is basically a story of technological horror, as Richard Vickers uses video cameras and television monitors to record the deaths. Wentworth is trapped into going along with Vickers's demands; he dies, as does Becky. Much of this portion is characterized by Leslie Nielson camping it up, humming "I'm just wild about Harry," rescuing Harry from the crab--a standard monster-ploy in traditional SF. (Incidentally, King notes that originally the crab was to attack Wentworth, but the real crabs came too close to hurting Danson, who was, after all, buried to the neck in sand and unable to protect himself). There is a sense of game-playing in the segment, but with an unsettling darker overtone.

In the second half, however, the film shifts genres, from the psychological games of "The Ledge" to the realm of the supernatural. Wentworth and Becky Vickers return. If the first half seems uniquely King, the second reflects Romero's hand. It is primarily a cinematic exercise, as the scene changes to night. Television monitors (black and white, to help the viewer differentiate between levels of presentation, levels of "reality") first show fog and mist, then shadows behind curtains. Then the horror gradually reveals itself. We see hands and arms of the creatures; in a self-reflexive moment, they pass the same ashtray used as murder weapon in "Father's Day," reminding us of both the crime and the vengeance of the earlier episode. Then we see shambling feet and dripping seaweed; finally the doors open and the walking dead stand revealed. They speak, and in a technique borrowed from "Father's Day" and "Jordy Verrill," their voices are distorted, suggesting their distancing from humanity. Vickers shoots; in a touch reminiscent of Romero's Night of the Living Dead trilogy, we see bullets tearing at undead flesh. The lighting in part disguises the blood bubbling from shattered eye sockets and torn flesh. Then the backgrounds shift to comic-book intensity as we see the victimizer made victim, in good E. C. fashion by suffering the same fate that he inflicted upon his victims.

The longest individual segment in Creepshow, and by far the most fully developed in terms of plot and character, is "The Crate." It is also the most graphic, with frequent recourse to blood and gore; again, however, the cinematic technique mutes and disguises that fact by shifting to stark red backdrops and red lighting at crucial moments--the blood in effect disappears, replaced by another block of color, as it were.

Still, the episode is unquestionably the most violent in the anthology. At least three people die bloody, on-screen deaths--four, if one counts Wilma Northrup's fantasy death when Harry Northrup "shoots" her to the polite applause of the faculty and wives in the early moments of the film. The remainder are victims of the monster in the crate, an appropriate image, since on a second level, the episode deals also with victims of another kind of monster.

In true King fashion, "The Crate" concentrates on Wilma as a monstrous woman, psychically if not physically, consuming and destroying those around her. Harry is her most obvious victim; Dexter Stanley is almost equally effected, however, and her actions at the faculty tea indicate her attitudes toward everyone at Horlicks Univer-

sity (not coincidentally where Michael and Regina
Cunningham teach in Christine and where Deke,
Randy, LaVerne, and Rachel might eventually have
graduated had they not gone for a late-October
swim in "The Raft"--it is, by definition, not a
nice place).

The plot opens by evoking chance; the janitor
flips a coin, which rolls behind a screen underneath a stairway. When he shines his light into
the darkness, he sees the crate. From that moment, the story moves inexorably through multiple
layers of death, culminating in the death of one
monster and the presumed destruction of the other.

The monster in the crate has an interesting
genesis. King talks of a real crate, found beneath
a stairway at the University of Maine in Orono:

> They were closing down the chemistry
> building and they found all this stuff,
> including a crate that had been under
> the stairs for about a hundred years.
> What got to me was the idea of a hundred
> years´ worth of students going up and
> down those stairs with the crate right
> underneath! It probably had nothing in
> it but old magazines, but it kind of
> tripped over in my mind that it could
> have been something really sinister in
> there. (Gagne, "Creepshow" 47)

The "something really sinister" he imagined for
the short story version of "The Crate" (Gallery,
July 1979) became, in the hands of Romero and
special effects designer Tom Savini a literaliza-
tion of the old comic-book Tasmanian devil--a
whirlwind composed of teeth and appetite.

Yet it is more than that. Writing on the
crate, faint with age, identifies the owner as
Julia Carpenter, a member of the 1834 Horlicks
University Arctic expedition. The inscription is
certainly an off-hand reference to John Carpenter,
whose own monster emerges from frozen wastes with
an equally voracious appetite for violence and
blood (The Thing, 1982), and whose original
inspiration came from John W. Campbell´s 1930´s
short story, "Who Goes There," published a neat
century after Julia Carpenter´s expedition.

As brought to "life" by Savini, the Arctic

creature is frightening enough for several films,
particularly since--in good horror tradition--we
see it at first only in fragments, in momentary
glimpses of eyes and teeth, enclosed by the dark
edges of the crate´s sides and top (powerful
examples, by the way, of careful cinematic closure
to insure that the viewers´ imaginations will move
well beyond the frames of vision actually provided). It is so convincing that Hal Holbrook reacted to it quite genuinely. Holbrook asked that
Romero not let him see the monster at all until he
was in front of the camera:

> George´s eyes lit up when he heard
> that. He knew I wanted to react honest-
> ly to the thing. So I turned my back
> when they rigged the crate. When George
> yelled "action," I spun around and this
> huge head popped out of the box. It was
> truly monstrous. My direction called
> for me to stagger backwards about six
> feet, hit a wall, and slump down. I
> tell you, I don´t even remember doing
> it, although it´s all on film. It came
> very instinctively.
> The monster was so real that it was
> easy to work with . Whenever I had to
> react to it for a close-up, I asked
> George to put the mock-up of the crea-
> ture off camera so I could stare at it.
> It was horrifying. It was disgusting.
> I loved it! (Naha, "Frontrow Seats" 49)

Technically, "The Crate" is one of the most
interesting episodes of Creepshow. It relies
heavily on framing--on scenes shot through hallway
doors, scenes cut diagonally by the stairway,
scenes outlined and restricted by the crate. The
red blood finds an effective visual counterpoint
in almost sterilely white halls, a technique also
used in the Prologue, in "Something To Tide You
Over," and archetypally in "They´re Creeping Up on
You." Backgrounds become vividly red abstractions
when the creature finally emerges, suggesting the
comic-book simplicity of representation and les-
sening the impact of the gore.
As edited by Paul Hirsch, it is a tight narrative, building tension on tension. In true

fairy-tale style, Hirsch uses every second; Harry Northrup just barely completes the initial clean-up when Wilma arrives. He hardly has a spare second to catch his breath. And, this time following the conventions of such horror films as The Blob, the episode concludes on a note of indeterminacy and irresolution: the creature (not Savini's mechanical, by the way, but a non-articulated mock-up) is dumped into an abandoned quarry, but we last see it breaking the crate and staring through a new framing device--presumably to escape and strike again. After all, we now have a new sequence of victim/victimizer and possibly a new level of vengeance.

The final segment concentrates on the theme of isolation. Upson Pratt, reclusive millionaire and tangential member of the human race, discovers what can happen when one treats other people as if they were insects. In this case, the instrument of revenge is insects--over 20,000 cockroaches, including several thousand four-inch specimens dug out of caves in Trinidad especially for the filming of Creepshow (most of the rest were purchased from a roach-supply house). In that sense, "They're Creeping Up on You" may be the most horrific of all, at least for anyone who shares Tom Savini's absolute dread of roaches.

Visually, the choice of insects was appropriate. The set as finally designed is starkly white; originally, the script called for an ornately Victorian period piece, until it was discovered that roaches let loose in a model of the set immediately disappeared underneath and behind the furnishings. Rethinking the problem, King and Romero decided on the stark sterility of unalleviated white, with as few furnishings as possible. The set not only allows for better control of the roaches (and there is no such thing as a "stunt" roach; they simply crawl wherever they want), but it also accentuates Pratt's moral darkness as we hear him dealing with people through the mediation of electronic devices: his telephone, and a distorting peephole in his front door.

The episode neatly defines the disparities between external and internal. Outside Pratt's window, we see a skyline, well-lit, suggesting business and human interaction; inside, we see

whiteness and blankness and inaction. E. G.
Marshall´s Upson Pratt is human on the surface;
inside, he is devious, coldly calculating, manipu-
lative, and as horrific as any monster we have
seen yet. He is both a cancer and a cockroach,
consuming lives as unthinkingly as he consumes his
cereal--or at least, until he pours a bowlful and
finds it alive with roaches. In good E. C. fashion, he must confront his deepest fear. A fanatic
about cleanliness, as testified to by the many
devices he uses to keep his sterile environment
precisely that way, he faces the epitome of the
unclean . . . thousands of cockroaches.

The closing effects for the segment are
particularly gruesome. The theme of internal
versus external literalizes as roaches pour from
Pratt´s lifeless body, erupting from his mouth and
chest. He becomes the insect he had assumed
others to be. The artificially white sterility in
which he has isolated and imprisoned himself
transforms into a heaving mass of organic, brown
movement--an image of the life he had denied
himself and everyone around him.

The final segment of Creepshow provides an
epilogue to all that has gone on before. Two
garbagemen (one played by special-effects director
Tom Savini, who notes that an item advertised in
the comic book is just an "effect") retrieve the
Creepshow comic book, thumb through it, and
discover that the coupon for an authentic voodoo
doll is missing. In a quick cut to the kitchen,
we see the father complaining about a stiff neck,
and the mother ironing. She picks up a shirt,
begins working on it, notices an oddly shaped hole
in the material, and tosses the shirt into a
basket. At this point it becomes clear what has
happened; the boy, played by King´s older son Joe,
has brought the world of Creepshow into his
reality. Vengeance is a force to be reckoned
with. In a final scene, the boy´s triumphant,
mephistophelean grin is transformed into yet
another comic-book frame, part of the larger
Creepshow that in fact contains all that we have
seen.

Frames within frames within frames, enclo-
sures enclosed, isolation made more isolating,
victimizers become victims, and vengeance visited
upon evil-doers--all of these are implicit in

Creepshow. As a film it is ultimately uneven. Some episodes work on entirely different levels from others; treatments vary from the broadly (almost painfully) comic to the supremely disgusting to the superlatively horrifying. Yet to say so is not to condemn the film, since that range of possibilities suggests precisely what King and Romero set out to create. Creepshow was intended as fun--but in a special, E. C. sense of the word. To that extent, it succeeds.

CHAPTER VII

Cujo (1983)

If the chapters in this book had subtitles, the most appropriate one for the discussion of Cujo might be "Happy Ending in Horrorland" or "Happy Ending in Hollywood."

In the film version of Cujo, Tad Trenton lives.

This fact is not necessarily a flaw in the film, however. Indeed, during a question-and-answer session at the Conference on the Fantastic (March 1984), one questioner asked King directly how he had reacted to the alteration. He answered that he felt good about it. In fact, he had originally intended that Tad would live.

> I thought all the time I wrote that book that the kid was going to live. I really did. I was sure he was going to live, there was no other ending for it. I knew that I would probably be crucified or something by the fans if the kid didn't live--they would say "How could you do that, how could you kill that little kid?" So he went through all these terrible things and I knew he was going to live, because it's impossible to put a kid through all that stuff in front of an audience and then say, "Here's the punchline, guys. He died."

Only at the end of the writing process, as he realized that Donna Trenton had been giving her son artificial respiration for fifteen minutes and he still was not breathing, did King himself understand that the boy had died. He considered revising the ending, then decided against it. After all, in this world, little boys do die; "there's crib death, there's childhood leukemia, brain tumors, cars, you name it" (Winter, "Art" 15). Still, King was probably relieved when Hollywood declared that Tad Trenton could live.

Of course, such a departure from the text means a fundamental change in the assumptions of the narrative itself, and such is indeed the case. The film Cujo differs from the novel, not so much in the surface level of plot as in the secondary levels of character and theme. The Trentons are less complex in the film, more readily understandable to their audience and to themselves. Tad moves further from the center, becoming more peripheral in a tale of a husband and a wife re-aligning themselves after a major disruption in their marriage.

In spite of the changes, however, the film paradoxically remains true to the novel. Perhaps this occurs because the novel itself is so aware of film and is structured around filmic qualities. Throughout, King refers to film for metaphors and images by which his characters can assess and understand their situations. Shortly after arriving at the Cambers' deserted farm, Donna Trenton steps out of the Pinto, sees Cujo, and freezes. Tad screams, freeing Donna from her paralysis and irritating Cujo's sensitive ears. The dog lunges at the car, strikes the window, and falls. Donna thinks that he has knocked himself out; then

> a moment later Cujo's foam-covered, twisted face popped up outside her window, only inches away, like a horror-movie monster that has decided to give the audience the ultimate thrill by coming right out of the screen. (156)

Later, Vic decides to return to Castle Rock. Roger Breakstone tries to dissuade him but Vic cannot be swayed:

> He was in motion now, and being in motion was better, but [a] feeling of unreality persisted. He kept having thoughts about movie sets, where what looks like Italian marble is really just Con-Tact paper, where all the rooms end just above the camera's sight line and where someone is always lurking in the background with a clapper board. Scene #41, Vic convinces Roger to Keep On Plugging, Take One. He was an actor and

this was some crazy absurdist film.
(260)

The reference to appearance and reality in
films provides a nice transition from the novel to
the film. As with most of King's narratives, Cujo
seems a natural for filming; indeed, more than
most, it invites a film translation. On a purely
pragmatic level, it is a more streamlined work
than most of King's novels. The novel boasts a
fairly limited cast, easily transferred to film.
At the center stand Vic, Donna, and Tad Trenton;
peripheral to them are Steve Kemp, the Cambers,
Gary Pervier, and Roger Breakstone. Although
there are of course additional characters in the
novel, these nine are sufficient for the narrative
as it develops in the film.

In addition, Cujo is characterized by limited
settings as well. To move from novel to film requires sets for the Trenton home, the Cambers, and
brief scenes at Kemp's and Pervier's. Additional
locales, such as the cemetery in the foreground as
Donna Trenton drives by in the Pinto, foreshadow
developments. In general, however, the film suggests only those few settings that contribute materially to the film.

The narrative also differs markedly from
King's, not only in the conclusion but also in the
inherent complexity. Subplots developed to great
depth in the novel are handled in a few short
scenes (the Sharps cereal debacle, for example) or
even in a line or two. Such a simplification is,
of course, expected in film versions of works as
long and as complex as King's. What remains, however, holds together more completely than happens
in many other King films. Salem's Lot as film
seems at times fragmented and disjointed; De
Palma's Carrie suffers from the loss of King's
documentary approach; Kubrick's The Shining
eliminated subplots ruthlessly, to the point that
the few reflections from King's vision--i.e., the
dog-faced character and the other masquers that
suddenly and inexplicably appear--have little
connection with the narrative as Kubrick has
enfleshed it.

In Cujo, on the other hand, the narrative
benefits from editing for film. The tapestry of
elements reduces to Donna and Tad being trapped in

the Pinto and Vic searching for them; everything
else becomes secondary. The affair between Donna
and Steve Kemp, for example, is of an entirely
different nature in the film; Vic knows the truth
even before he confronts Donna, since he has seen
her with Kemp. The affair becomes less a subplot
than a filmic device for insuring that certain
characters show up at specific places to impel the
narrative movement.

In line with these characteristics, the novel
also suggests mainstream fiction more completely
than most of King´s works. It reads, as one critic has suggested, more like a Bachman novel than a
King--that is, the elements of supernatural horror
are touched upon lightly. The novel´s monster in
the closet does not develop fully, and hints of a
connection between Cujo and Frank Dodd were actually added to later drafts. In the film, even
those ephemeral connections have disappeared. The
film concentrates on a realistic narrative: a woman and her child trapped by a rabid St. Bernard.
The monster in the closet almost disappears from
the film; only in the opening scenes does the film
create a sense of fear focused on the closet.

Each of these elements--the limited cast and
setting, the straight-line narrative, the mainstream tenor--works to director Lewis Teague´s ad-
vantage. Instead of making an abortive attempt at
reproducing all of King´s novel, Teague concentrates on the essence of the narrative, focusing
rather than altering, with the exception of the
conclusion, of course. As a result, the film is
both recognizably King´s novel and a coherent film
in its own right. Having read the novel helps in
understanding the film; it is not, however, necessary to understanding it.

Teague´s direction and Jan de Bont´s photography define a pervasive theme in the film by ac-
centuating the fluidity of perception throughout,
examining visual perspectives as the film explores
psychological, emotional, and physical perspectives as well. One of the most impressive technical elements in the film, in fact, relates to
camera angles as images of perception.

The opening shots establish a particular
mood: open fields, a rabbit nosing through tall
grass. Then suddenly the mood changes as we see
first the rabbit, caught in the frame of a low-

angle camera. As the camera swivels slowly, Cujo´s leg appears, and at first we are not quite sure what the intrusive element is. (In a nice bit of foreshadowing, we also see a string of saliva dropping from the dog´s muzzle.) The camera is low to the ground, subtly emphasizing Cujo´s size and mass.

During the credits, the scene remains playful. The dog chases the rabbit; the rabbit ducks and dodges; it doesn´t seem as if either is in deadly peril. As the Sharps cereal professor might say, "Nope, nothing wrong here."

Then the credits stop as the rabbit drops into the cave, followed by as much of Cujo as the dog can manage.

With the change in setting, the camera angles and lighting change also. The cave is eerily lit, with one long shot of just the dog´s head caught high up in the wall. His barking disturbs the bats, which attack. The camera now shifts to close-up, as the rabid bat bites Cujo, setting in motion the primary movement of the film. Then we have a brief respite as the remaining credits roll.

Almost immediately, however, we are again thrust into an eerie scene, this time Tad Trenton´s bedroom. His closet stands open; he must cross the room and turn out the light, then run safely back to bed before the monster can get him. In this single episode, Teague uses slow-motion photography and overhead camera shots angled down at Tad´s bed to create a distorted view of the room. Yet another camera angle results in the illusion that Tad´s bed (and thus, for him, safety) lies unreachably distant from the light switch. And even when the boy reaches the security of the bed, there is one final camera manipulation--a distant shot of Tad slowly zooms in to focus on a close-up of his face, white with fear and surrounded by the darkness and shadows of his room.

From then on, Cujo relies heavily on manipulating camera angles and camera movement to communicate tone, atmosphere, and theme. Rarely does the camera focus directly at objects; more frequently (or at least more noticeably) it shoots up or down, creating fascinating and insightful false perspectives.

At times, the camera concentrates on con-
flicting layers of reality. Again and again, particularly with Donna and Tad Trenton inside the
Pinto, the camera stands external to their "reality," and defines them in the context of an outer
layer. We see the characters through their car
windows; yet those same windows simultaneously
reflect an alternate world of pastoral-seeming
trees. At times, the reflections almost obscure
the two people trapped in the car. What is in
fact an epitome of terror is screened by an illusion of peaceful, pastoral nature.

At other times, the camera shifts to circles
of reality, rather than layers. The camera will
circle slowly, gradually but inexorably widening
the viewer's field of vision, including into the
scene elements that alter the context. There is
little documentary sense here, little use of a
fixed camera that attempts for cinematic neutral-
ity. Instead, the camera becomes almost a character, circling into scene with smoothly fluid
movements, then widening our awareness of other
elments in that scene, initially just beyond our
view. As it moves, it creates ever-expanding
circles that define the complex relationships in
the film as well as the widening circles of fear
and error.

Again, the best examples occur in those scene
with Donna and Tad at the Camber farm. The camera
will begin focused on the two characters, then
begin circling . . . and suddenly the foam- and
blood-spattered head of the rabid dog will intrude
into the shot, emphasizing an external horror
imposed upon them. In one instance, the circling
camera goes beyond just including additional
elements. As Donna and Tad weaken from heat,
dehydration, and fear, the camera circles from
mother to son, son to mother, completing a 360°
circle--and then continues to circle, faster and
faster, showing first Donna, then Tad, then Donna
again, with the emptiness of the Camber farm
spinning by outside. The camera seems to communicate its own message: there is no escape from this
terror.

A third specific technique in Cujo relates
both to camera angles and to the underlying prem-
ises of horror film discussed in earlier chapters.
In addition to layering and circling, the camera

also frames. We see only a selected portion of reality; the rest remains for our imagination to fill in. Frequently throughout the film, <u>something</u> stands between the viewer and the characters. The effect is a visual limiting that parallels other kinds of limitations: our inability to know, understand, and "see" the characters fully here becomes literalized. We see as incomplete and distorted a world as the characters themselves do, as when Vic realizes that his wife is having an affair, but cannot "see" far enough into her and into her life to understand either why she began or why such an affair could never last long.

The "somethings" that intrude between characters and their understanding of reality--and between viewers and their full visual apprehension of the film's images--parallel other unnameable foci of fear in the narrative: the things that fragment marriages, both the Trentons' and the Cambers'; the things that destroy individual's lives, either the purposelessness of a Steve Kemp, or the drunken cynicism of a Gary Pervier; the things that change a family pet into a deadly monster; and the things that hide in children's closets by night and bring fear and terror instead of sleep.

Again and again, "things" intrude to block vision. As the Trenton's car drives into the Cambers' yard, we see the car fragmented through broken fencing. We see Pervier's body through the frame of a claustrophobically narrow corridor; Camber sees the rabid dog through the frame of an open doorway. At other times, we must peer around door jambs, car frames, ceiling beams, steering wheels, car seats; behind these objects, only partially visible, lie the true objects of our attention, our empathy, or our fear. In a moment of particular tension, Donna Trenton steps out of the battered Pinto. She cannot see the dog. The camera shifts, and we see <u>her</u> feet, framed between the Pinto's undercarriage and the rough ground, and we see them from Cujo's perspective as he crouches on the other side of the car. Then Donna crouches down and looks beneath the car. Now we see the opposite view, again framed by car and ground, and there is nothing there. She stands, half turns, and the dog attacks her from behind the camera itself, suddenly appearing through the right-hand frame.

Even when the camera allows a straight-on view of characters, it manipulates perspective and perception. In one powerful moment, as Donna and Tad are suffering inside the Pinto, she holds the boy on her lap. She stares straight ahead, unmoving; he seems either asleep or unconscious. The camera, however, catches the two at just the proper moment to create a cinematic parallel to Michelangelo's Pieta, an image the camera accentuates as it follows the line of Tad's leg and finally stops, focusing on the boy's foot.

All of these techniques create a sense of inexorable movement. When the plot slows momentarily, Teague continues to shift camera angles, even within individual scenes and episodes, constantly distorting the perspectives afforded the viewers. We see common things through new frames of reference; and the common things suddenly become imbued with fear and terror. At the same time, the camera constantly creates barriers between what is and what individuals can see and understand.

To concentrate this much on the techniques of camera angle might suggest that Cujo is intended as an "artsy" films; such is, of course, not the case. Teague's fluid approach to visual perception in fact emphasizes the relationships he hopes to capture on film, as well as helping to define the characters whose lives he follows.

Those characters are frequently faithful to the intent, if not to the words of King's novel. Dee Wallace's Donna Trenton clearly begins as a bored, quietly frustrated, guiltily unfaithful wife and mother; later, trapped in the Pinto, she convincingly moves through a range of emotions, beginning with irritation and ending with selfless, murderous rage directed against the dog. In a particularly apt moment, she in effect calls down her own doom. After waiting in the Cambers' yard for some time, she tries to start the Pinto. She turns the key; the engine catches and the car moves slowly forward, out of danger. Then, impulsive and expressive, she stops to curse the dog--and the car stalls. Cinematically, at least, she creates the context for the climax of the film.

Daniel Hugh-Kelly at first seems too young to play Vic Trenton. He is too full of youthful high

spirits, not vain or self-centered enough to
represent King's character accurately. But with
the streamlining of plot in the screenplay, Vic
Trenton changes, and Hugh-Kelly does in fact grow
into the part. Since Donna is still sleeping with
Steve Kemp at the beginning of the action--and
since Vic sees them together, thus eliminating the
need for a complicated flashback--Vic's emotions
and responses can be more direct in the film than
in the novel. His reactions are also colored by
the fact that he is more closely acquainted with
Kemp in the film as well; they are apparently
frequent tennis partners. Thus his reactions do
not require a poison-pen letter as motivation. As
with other elements of the film, his character
becomes more direct, more action-oriented.

Danny Pintauro is appealing as Tad Trenton,
effectively suggesting the incremental terror at
the heart of the novel and the film. Other characters, more peripheral, also work well. Ed
Lauter's Joe Camber is convincingly brutal and
harsh; Mills Watson's Gary Pervier equally convincingly self-centered and cynical. Brett Camber
(Billy Jacoby) seems a bit too old; his mother
(Kaiulani Lee) correspondingly too young, inherently more attractive than King's Charity Camber.
But with the alterations in plot, both characters
have lost much of their importance; they serve
primarily to define who Cujo is and what he becomes.

One addiional character deserves mention.
Sandy Ward plays Sheriff Bannerman, an elderly man
wearing a police uniform. He appears late in the
film, goes to the Camber farm, and discovers the
bloody and battered Pinto. He begins to call for
back-up help, hears an odd noise, then breaks off
his call to investigate. He finds Cujo, and dies.
Unfortunately, the film version of Cujo appeared
prior to Cronenberg's Dead Zone, in which Bannerman appears in a much stronger, more central role.
Early viewers of the film might have seen nothing
inherently wrong with the representation of the
sheriff; later viewers, those watching both films
on videocassette, for example, will find Cujo's
Bannerman almost a throw-away character, poorly
developed, and certainly not the same man that Tom
Skerritt would portray a year later in
Cronenberg's film. In fact, only after his death

does Vic refer to him as "Bannerman."

The final character deserving mention is, of course, Cujo himself. The dog is highly effective, particularly as the rabies progresses and the dog's coat becomes damp and matted with dirt and blood. When the animal throws itself against th Pinto, there is an eminently believable sense of mass and weight determined to get at, and kill, the woman and boy. What is missing, however, is any inherent connection between the dog and the monster in the closet. In the novel, that connection, however tenuous, is at least suggested; references to Frank Dodd from The Dead Zone hint that whatever is in the closet (and there is something; Vic feels its presence and smells it as well) has also partially inhabited the rabid dog. In the film, the monster in the closet and the dog remain essentially unrelated; there is no reference to Dodd at all. Vic enters the closet at the critical moment, but neither hears Tad's voice no perceives anything out of the ordinary.

In fact, the only hint that Cujo might in some way be a monster occurs when Donna Trenton attacks the dog with the baseball bat. The bat splinters, and when Cujo leaps on her, the splintered remnant enters his chest. In the novel, the wood enters the dogs eye and brain, images of intellect. Paradoxically, Donna loses control of intellect and succumbs to the irrational and emotional, beating the dead dog's corpse and inadvertantly allowing her son to die; the moments wasted might have been enough to save Tad.

In the film, the stake through the heart suggests that Donna is killing a vampire; and certainly the dog's subsequent appearance relates more closely to the last-moment shock of the bloody hand in Carrie or the Reverend Lowe's final lunge in Silver Bullet than to the kind of realistic film Cujo had become. The dog's bursting through the kitchen window is almost gratuitously horrific, in the most stereotypic sense.

The final scene is the epitome of Cujo. Tad lives. Cujo dies. Donna regains her ability to act, to protect and defend. Vic arrives--late, as seems usual for him throughout their relationship--but he does. And the nuclear family, reunited at last, stands on the Camber porch as the closing credits begin.

As a film, _Cujo_ seems intermediate. It avoids the excesses of _Salem's Lot_ and the idiosyncratic approach of Kubrick's _The Shining_. It modifies King's narrative to fit the restraints of a two-hour film, but avoids as much as possible altering the characters and situations without reason. The dialogue remains true to the novel, as do characters and settings. At the same time, it has lost the sharpness of King's prose, the indefinable element that his references to Castle Rock and Frank Dodd brought the novel. It has, in fact, become an exploration of true horror, the horror we may confront at any time. There are no vampires or haunted hotels or psychokinetic adolescents in _Cujo_; there is only a big, friendly dog that contracts rabies, or a wife who makes a mistake and risks losing her husband, or a little boy terrified of shadows who nearly dies.

But he doesn't--and that may be the final strength of _Cujo_.

In Teague's vision, the family survives.

CHAPTER VIII

Dead Zone (1983)

James Verniere begins his preview of the film version of Dead Zone (with the article deleted) by arguing that here "is where novelist Stephen King and filmmaker David Cronenberg will either come together in glory or cancel each other out" (55).

Fortunately, in the opinion of most viewers, the first occurred.

Along with Carrie and Cujo, Dead Zone consistently places high on lists defining which of the films made from King's works are most effective. Certainly it is more effective, both as film and as novel adaptation, than Children of the Corn, for example, and less idiosyncratic than The Shining. It retains the tone and atmosphere of King's novel, yet avoids the passionless translation of Firestarter.

A good deal of the credit for Dead Zone's success lies directly with David Cronenberg's approach to the project.

Originally, Lorimar purchased film rights to the novel, intending to hire Sidney Pollack as producer. The first choice for director was Stanley Donen, whose credits include Singin' in the Rain, Seven Brides for Seven Brothers, Royal Wedding, Charade, The Little Prince, Bedazzled, and Saturn 3. Donen apparently intended to approach the narrative externally, with the resulting film as objective and realistic as possible.

Stephen King was asked for a screenplay, which he completed and delivered. Shortly thereafter, however, when Lorimar phased out its feature-film division, the project languished until rights were picked up a year later by Dino de Laurentiis. He rejected King's script, assigning Andrei Konchalavsky to prepare an alternate. That script was not accepted, and de Laurentiis turned to Jeffrey Boam, whose screenplay ultimately formed the basis for the film.

Ten days after the release of Videodrome, David Cronenberg began work as the director of

Dead Zone, bringing with him an entirely different approach to film. Cronenberg has, as Verniere writes, developed virtually his own form of film, a "kind of cinema of pathology in which the ultimate horror is the horror of a diseased psyche" (55). His earlier films explored the possibilities of a mind-body duality that expressed itself in overt, graphic horror. Stereo (1969), Crimes of the Future (1970), Shivers (1975; his first commercial film), Rabid (1976), The Brood (1979), Scanners (1980), and Videodrome (1982) were characterized by increasing violence, horror, and graphic gore. Even while working on Dead Zone, in fact, Cronenberg was forced to re-edit portions of Videodrome to alter its rating from "X" to "R." William Beard says of horror films that they are, as a form,

> a symbolic treatment of ordinary human conflicts, and the horrific aspects of them are specifically symbolic of the psychological violence of the struggle. In Cronenberg's work the particular ordinary human conflict is the central question of emotional involvement as such: whether it is desirable, how it relates to instinct, what its consequences are and what are the consequences of its lack. (Handling 74)

In the earlier films, the "symbolic treatment" took form in images of horror, culminating in exploding heads in Scanners and equally graphic physical effects in Videodrome.

In addition, Cronenberg's plots and characters differed widely from what King's readers might be used to. King's power depends on his ability to put ordinary people into extraordinary situations; the situations bring the readers into the text, while the realistically drawn characters keep the readers there, forcing empathy under highly unusual circumstances. Cronenberg's earlier films worked from an opposite direction. His characters were, he noted, usually "strange, bizarre, or unusual--twisted, perhaps" (Verniere 56). Certainly viewers coming out of either Scanners or Videodrome might see how Cronenberg could handle Greg Stillson's psychotic irrationality; they might also, and justifiably, wonder how Cronenberg would handle the sensitivity of a Johnny Smith.

And yet, Cronenberg's vision brought something essential to Dead Zone, an introverted intensity in the characterization of Johnny Smith that gives the film greater power than it might otherwise have possessed. Even as it diverges from King's text, it does so in the right directions, defining Johnny Smith's isolation, his increasing reclusivity, his alienation from humanity. And more critically, Cronenberg consciously attempted to soften the impact of horrific images in the final film. He rejected King's screenplay as too brutal; it opened with Stillson torturing a young boy and emphasized the Castle Rock killer throughout. Although Cronenberg did introduce his own visions of horror into Dead Zone--most explicitly the suicide of Frank Dodd, "in terms of nasty imagery . . . probably the centerpiece of the movie," according to Cronenberg (Verniere 58)--the film as released is remarkably restrained, considering its director's antecedents. He specifically deleted, for example, the scene in which Stillson brutally kicks a dog to death, incorporated into King's screenplay.

In spite of such superficial differences, however, Cronenberg and King seem a fine match in Dead Zone. Verniere argues that where "Cronenberg is introspective, Stephen King is locomotive" (56); that is, Cronenberg moves through lyricism and image, whereas King moves through break-neck narrative and powerful episodes. There is an element of truth in Verniere's comment, of course, but it is also misleading. Dead Zone represents a median between the two extremes, for both Cronenberg and King. It is the most carefully tempered of King's novels, the most introspective. Its plotting is more episodic than anything else, complicated only by the interwoven strands of Johnny Smith's life and Stillson's rise to political power. Otherwise, the novel breaks into several distinct sections, each dealing with one facet of Johnny Smith's attempts to deal with his powers. More than other King novels (and more than several of the "Bachman" books), The Dead Zone is mainstream, touching only tangentially on the supernatural or horror. Johnny Smith is among

93

King's most memorable characters because he is so
much like Everyman . . . with one devastating
exception.

Cronenberg's film moves in the same direc-
tion--toward mainstream, humane drama, with as
light a touch of horror as possible. Initially,
Cronenberg felt strongly that his function was not
to re-write King's novel. "I'm not trying to make
the film be something that it's not," he said in
an interview. That, he stressed, was "a mistake
Stanley Kubrick made with The Shining. I've tried
to be faithful to the tone of the book and to
Stephen's voice" (Verniere 56). To a remarkable
extent, Cronenberg succeeded in both, while retaining his independent identity as artist and
filmmaker. Dead Zone is a tribute to the creative
energies of two very different men working in two
very different media.

In spite of superficial arguments to the contrary, King's novel provided a perfect vehicle for
Cronenberg. Tim Lucas notes that

> The Dead Zone isn't really a horror nov-
> el at all; it rather (in close approxi-
> mation with Cronenberg's own direction
> as a film maker and storyteller) tells a
> mainstream story in which the worlds of
> Mind and Imagination play an intrinsic,
> almost physical role. (25)

Mind and Imagination--the two components of Johnny
Smith that defy clear definition, and two continuing threads throughout Cronenberg's film career.

Nor are they the only connections. Mind and
body also enter in--two more elements that blend
to create an intensely empathetic character trapped in situations not of his choosing and out of
his control. In both novel and film, Johnny
Smith's physical state inversely parallels his
mental state; as his powers amplify, his physical
condition deteriorates. In the novel, King uses
the image of a tumor--the source of the blind
spot, the "dead zone" that persists in Johnny
Smith's visions. In the film, Cronenberg dispenses with the tumor and relies on external, visual parallels instead. As the powers grow, Johnny
becomes physically more fragile: his face ages,
his eyes become more deeply set and shadowed, his

expression haunted. Using the gift, he says, is "like dyin' inside." As in the novel, he is transformed into a man aware of his own mortality and yet forced to expend his life in order to protect and preserve others.

One of the earliest suggestions of changes in the narrative and of Cronenberg's commitment to retaining the flavor of King's original occurs as Johnny Smith and Sarah Bracknell go to the carnival just prior to the accident. In the novel, King introduces two key images: the mask and the Wheel of Fortune. In various guises, both will recur throughout the novel, culminating with the "unmasking" of Greg Stillson and the destruction of his political hopes. Both images are powerful and well developed in King's prose; unfortunately, they would be virtually impossible to incorporate as visual images, since so much depends upon how characters interpret them.

Cronenberg resolves the difficulty by substituting an image, much as Kubrick did with the maze in The Shining. The rollercoaster becomes Cronenberg's visual representation of chance, fortune, and the future. Its erratic movements, its lurching ups and downs, characterize the episodes of Dead Zone, paralleling Johnny Smith's own life. Most critically, only Johnny and Sarah ride the coaster; the remaining seats are empty, suggesting that the two people will be inextricably tied together, although not in ways either of them can predict.

That suggestion also makes more understandable another major change in the plot. As originally scripted, the child in the final scene was to have been simply the child of an onlooker. In terms of the novel, such a decision was wholly justified. Johnny had made his peace with his past, had accepted Sarah's present without him; there would have been no justification, therefore, for bringing her into the final scene.

During a rehearsal, however, Christopher Walken took aim with his rifle, then jokingly called out, "That's Denny. I can't shoot." Cronenberg liked the idea and searched for a child-actor who resembled the infant Denny nine months later, bringing Johnny's life full circle within the context of the film. He and Sarah share another rollercoaster--this one figurative,

95

rather than literal, and afflicting emotional
rather than physical balance. Johnny hesitates as
Stillson holds the child as a shield, and his hes-
itation kills him. In terms of King´s novel, such
an ending hints of Hollywood--everything seems too
pat, too neat. But given Cronenberg´s initial
imagery, perhaps there is more to it than at first
seems apparent.

In another minor but important addition to
King´s narrative, Cronenberg interweaves quota-
tions from Poe into crucial scenes--Johnny´s last
class, and his tutoring session just before Sarah
appears on his doorstep stumping for Stillson.
The final lines of "The Raven," with their
insistently repeated "Nevermore," are a highly
appropriate leitmotif for the entire film; and the
reference to the lost "Leonore" emphasizes the
true relationship between Johnny and Sarah. They
will meet again, but, as she says after their day
together at Herb Smith´s farm, "not like today."

Cronenberg treats King´s narrative with great
respect. He selects the four or five critical
episodes and re-creates them, remaining true to
their intent and substance rather than to the ac-
cidents of detail. In at least one case, he alters the episode almost out of recognition, yet in
doing so makes the film stronger. In the novel,
Chris Stuart is eighteen years old, an athlete
afraid of failing his college admissions examina-
tions. He is threatened with death in a roadhouse
fire. In the film, he is closer to ten or eleven,
an introspective loner, much as Johnny Smith must
have been as a child.

Cronenberg rejected most of the episode. Although he erroneously refers to a gym fire in The
Dead Zone and connects it unfairly with Carrie,
his main point remains valid--to use a teenaged
Chris would introduce "the whole high school/
teenage thing," a theme he considered to have been
"done to death." According to the interview, in
fact, "Stephen said that he would´ve done the book
our way, if he had thought of it" (Lucas 60).

Reworking the episode to include only four or
five boys in a hockey accident might have been a
response to budgetary restraints; obviously it
would be easier and more economical to stage than
a major fire requiring hundreds of extras. Beyond
this pragmatic approach, however, lies the una-

voidable fact that the younger Chris creates a depth of empathy for Johnny Smith, as does Anthony Zerbe's far more limited Roger Stuart, with his clearly defined choice between belief and disbelief. He chooses wrongly; the film is far more explicit about his guilt than was the novel. Nor does he play any subsequent role, as he does in the novel. Johnny Smith never speaks to either Chris or Roger Stuart again in the film. That portion of his life is past; he becomes even more isolated, in preparation for his final sacrifice in defeating the evil that is Greg Stillson.

Mentioning Zerbe's portrayal of Roger Stuart suggests another clear strength in Cronenberg's Dead Zone: casting. For the first time, Cronenberg was able to work with a full cast of experienced actors; and for the first time, one of King's novels would benefit also from such a cast. In spite of occasionally strong performances in previous films, casting had been a weak spot for most of the films made from King's novels. Nicholson's eccentric Jack Torrance, Duvall's equally eccentric Wendy Torrance, David Soul's aenemic and slightly hysterical Ben Mears--such screen performances resulted more in criticism than in appreciation.

With Dead Zone, however, primary and secondary characters fit their roles. Christopher Walken is uncannily convincing as Johnny Smith as he changes through all of his physical states. Cronenberg credited much of the success in moving from novel to film to Walken's performance: "He's added part of himself to the character. Our portrait is very different from the book" (Verniere 56). It is difficult to overstate Walken's effect as the ethereally fragile Johnny Smith, occasionally frustrated by his life, occasionally crushed by the weight of responsibility his power brings. Everything from his hairstyle to his mode of dressing to his suggestion of pain in every physical movement defines Johnny's character, making inevitable his final choices. When he does resort to physical violence--destroying a vase in Roger Stuart's home to punctuate his warning about the hockey game, or firing at Stillson at the rally--it is so surprising that the act itself shocks more deeply than it would otherwise. In every respect, Walken's portrayal is Johnny Smith.

97

Much the same may be said for other members of the cast. Martin Sheen is brilliant as Greg Stillson, imbuing his performance with a subtle and sublimated threat. When Sonny Ellman breaks Johnny's grip and pulls Stillson away during the rally, Sheen's wordless glance conveys more than pages of dialogue could from a lesser actor. In a role that might threaten to overpower Walken's understated and introverted Johnny Smith, Sheen carefully keeps the extroverted and occasionally irrational Stillson just under control. As a counterforce to Johnny Smith, his Stillson makes up for the lack of parallel development that plays such an important part in the novel. Although Cronenberg wanted to keep the parallelism, he discovered that there was no way to orchestrate such a structure; instead, he settled for introducing Stillson late in the film, already well on his way to a Senate seat. Only indirectly--and through the nuances of Sheen's performance--do viewers understand the madness behind Stillson's drive; when Stillson and Ellman confront a recalcitrant newspaper editor and reveal their true characters, it comes as no real surprise. By the final scenes, Stillson represents a proper opponent for Johnny Smith, one whose pretensions are sufficiently dangerous to justify Johnny's voluntary death.

Brooke Adams is an appealing Sarah, slightly confused at the situation she finds herself in, yet taking it with as much equanimity as possible. Similarly, two veteran Canadian actors, Sean Sullivan and Jackie Burroughs, bring Herb and Vera Smith to life with small gestures and carefully timed delivery. Much of the visual impact of the film rests in art designer Carol Spier's attempts to create a mythical New England rather than a realistic New England. To achieve that effect, she (and others on the production staff) studied the art of Norman Rockwell. Niagara-on-the-Lake, Ontario, was selected for a filming site not because it resembled New England but because it resembles so strongly the idealized image of New England perpetuated by Rockwell. Sullivan seems as if he could have walked right out of a Rockwell painting, while the campaign posters for Greg Stillson were designed in the manner of Rockwell's paintings for Eisenhower's campaign (Lucas, "David Cronenberg's Dead Zone" 29).

Tom Skerrit brings much more credit to Sheriff Bannerman than did Sandy Ward in Cujo. Cronenberg initially hoped to use Hal Holbrook in the role; de Laurentiis (who retained control of casting) demurred. As a second choice, Skerrit proved valuable, bringing a sense of determination to the role that helped establish Bannerman's credibility. With only a few moments on screen, Skerrit managed to convey much of the anger, pent-up frustration, and fear that King spent pages developing in the novel.

Similarly, Nicholas Campbell's Frank Dodd makes the most out of a few seconds on screen, hinting at the insanity beneath an unusually innocent, naive-seeming face. His suicide is, as Cronenberg stated, particularly gruesome, one of the few suggestions in Dead Zone of Cronenberg's visual effects in earlier, more horrific films. Yet Campbell manages to made the brutality of the scene understandable. Although allowed even briefer screen time, Colleen Dewhurst, as Dodd's mother, demonstrates with brutal clarity why her son is insane.

Almost every character in the film brings to his or her role an authenticity that subsumes personal identity to the character portrayed. As a result, Dead Zone convinces on multiple levels, an achievement attained by few adaptations of King's works.

In part, the success of Dead Zone lies also with the fundamental assumptions shared by director Cronenberg, screenwriter Jeffrey Boam, and the rest of the production crew. This was not to be just another monster film, just another slasher film focusing on psychotic outsiders. Boam's script carefully defines a triptych of episodes (Lucas, "David Cronenberg's Dead Zone" 26-27). The first third concentrates on the accident and Johnny Smith's reactions to his new-found gift--in this case, withdrawing from it, refusing to accept what has happened to him. The second third shifts to the Castle Rock killer, signaled by Johnny Smith's voluntary decision to help Bannerman; he steps outside himself for the first time and uses his powers consciously to save lives. The third part deals with the increasing conflict between Johnny Smith and Greg Stillson, with the Stuart episodes more preparatory for the final confrontation than implicitly important. In this final third, Johnny Smith acts, realizing at last that his power is not a curse but a gift and that through it, he can indeed make a difference.

Boam's emphasis on Johnny Smith's gradual acceptance of the responsibilities his power entails in fact led Boam to say that King

> missed the point of his own book--namely, the conflict of Good and Evil, and the notion that decent people have responsibilities to their fellow man even if they won't admit it and don't like it." (Lucas, "David Cronenberg's Dead Zone" 27)

Greg Stillson becomes little more than a symbol for internal changes in Johnny Smith who, as his name implies, is a common man caught in uncommon circumstances. As he learns the nature of his power and accepts it, he also learns to move beyond himself, to act in behalf of others.

Seen in that light, Dead Zone is indeed not a horror film, a fact that de Laurentiis discovered just before publicity for the film's release began. Re-working original plans to sell the film as a horror film, based on a novel by America's premier horror writer, directed by an important name in horror film, scheduled for release just before Halloween, de Laurentiis concentrated instead on the human drama--and humane drama--of the film. It is to his credit that he did so; and it is to the credit of Cronenberg and his production crew that Dead Zone merited such treatment.

CHAPTER IX

Christine (1983)

Christine was the fourth Stephen King film released in two years, following Creepshow (1982), Cujo (1983) and Dead Zone (1983). It also represented the most rapidly produced film from a King text. Shooting began within days of the novel's publication, and the film was released within a year.

For these and other reasons, Christine confronted more disapproval--even before it was released--than earlier films. It all seemed too quick, too pat, too obviously a set-up for King to benefit from yet another movie tie-in.

Even worse, the novel itself, while rapidly attaining best-seller status, was as frequently disparaged as the resulting film. Reviewers such as David G. Hogan spoke in disapproving terms of both:

> Stephen King's entertaining novel (his pulpiest and most unabashedly silly) should have been sure-fire movie material. The book features a very tuff car, lots of rock 'n roll lyrics and appealing teenagers who struggle against the evil that threatens to destroy them. Director John Carpenter--fresh from being burned in his abortive attempt to film King's Firestarter--seemed a logical choice to undertake Christine. If nothing else, King's shaggy sedan story would assure Carpenter of a box-office hit and repair some of the damage done by the flop of The Thing. ("Carpenter Borrowed King's Car" 56)

According to Hogan and others, the film was clearly flawed. Hogan pointed to characterization in the film as the primary difficulty. Although individual actors are talented and highly competent, they are not allowed to express their char-

acters fully, largely because of Carpenter´s direction. Keith Gordon´s Arnie Cunningham receives
particular attention. Gordon is physically appropriate for the role--"small, dark and intense--a
frustrated romantic trapped in an uncaring world"
(Hogan 56). His association/obsession with Christine alters him, changes suggested externally by
greater physical security, a swaggering grace paralleling his increasingly sophisticated wardrobe.
His black, horn-rimmed, nerd-like glasses, broken
in the initial encounter with Buddy Repperton and
stereotypically mended with white tape, disappear;
Gordon´s eyes certainly communicate an internal
intensity that gives his representation of Arnie
Cunningham greater strength.
   At this point, Hogan argues, we expect to see
Arnie struggle against the growing obsession, acknowledging to himself at least the evil that
threatens to overcome him:

> But Arnie doesn´t struggle. The narra-
> tive doesn´t allow him any time to re-
> sist. Arnie becomes Joe Cool in a wink
> and a howling demon minutes later.
> There is no dramatic tension: Arnie just
> changes.
>   Because we do not observe the boy´s
> fight to remain as he is (as King allow-
> ed us to do), Arnie is not a sympathetic
> victim but just a disagreeable brute who
> cuffs his new girlfriend . . . , roughs
> up his dad and litters the highway with
> beer cans. (Hogan 56)

   In large measure, Hogan has pinpointed one of
the most glaring problems in the film. My first
viewing of Christine resulted in precisely the
same question, the same sense of having been
cheated of scenes that would have lent the film
tremendous power. Arnie does not struggle; he is
not allowed to enter into the viewer´s imagination
as he did in the novel. Things move far too
quickly, as when he suddenly appears at the
football game with Leigh Cabot (Alexandra Paul) in
tow; the last word we had from her was that she
was not interested in dating. We do not see how
or when or why Arnie and Leigh meet and decide to
date. Their relationship seems superficial

throughout the film, since Carpenter has decided not to give any foundation for it. Consequently, when Leigh turns to Dennis Guilder (John Stockwell) for help, her actions are far less tragic and poignant than in the novel. There seems to be little agonizing on her part (or Dennis's) over a lost friend.

Even more critically, Arnie receives blame in the film for Christine's murderous actions. Although partially exonerated for several of the early murders, Arnie does not have alibis for all of them. This ambivalence toward Arnie increases as the film moves to its climax. In the novel, it is clear that Arnie is not responsible directly for any of the killings. King carefully removes Arnie and his mother, sending them on a trip to visit a distant university at the same time that Christine attacks Dennis and Leigh in Darnell's garage. And, in a development that provides a provisionally acceptable resolution to Arnie's obsession, he is killed under circumstances that suggest his final rejection of Christine's evil powers and his willingness to confront Le Bay's ghost.

In the film, on the other hand, Arnie becomes directly responsible for nearly killing Dennis and Leigh--or at least for tacitly acceding to their deaths. Christine appears in the garage and begins her attack on the two, much as in King's novel. In a scene not in the text, she crashes through the wall into Darnell's office, stops suddenly, and throws Arnie through the windshield, his dying body falling next to Leigh. A shard of glass has perforated his chest cavity, obviously killing him; he is both victimizer and victim, falling prey to his own obsession. The cinematic effect of his body hurtling from the car and the ghastly makeup intended to convince the viewers that he is dead eliminated any possible sympathy (let alone empathy) viewers might once have held for him. Regardless of whether he controlled Christine or was merely a passenger, his physical presence in the garage implicates him in her evil.

In defense of Carpenter's treatment of Arnie, L. Christine Harper argued that "Keith Gordon's transformation from nerd to normal to crazed is handled very well within the confines of the script" ("Reel Futures"). As she suggests, the

constraints of time limited much of what Carpenter
was able to do in the film. Even when the film
shows critical episodes, however, Arnie's character appears static, changed from when we last saw
it, but never in the process of change.   Hogan
refers to the Thanksgiving scene, a tremendously
important scene in the novel, since it represents
the last time Arnie and Dennis enjoy a friendship
undistorted by Christine's overt evil.   His own
personality is not yet submerged by Christine's
power or by Le Bay's ghostly presence.   The episode is quietly touching, a moment of peace before
the breaking storm.

     In the film, however, the scene is truncated,
emphasizing not the ending of a relationship but
Arnie's transformation into a new character.   The
scene is a "dramatic zero. It's Bad Arnie that's
come to visit. When the boy leaves the room, we
are neither upset nor moved, but merely relieved"
(Hogan 56).

     There are other weaknesses in the film as
well. Harper refers to a storyline that moves too
simply and directly through complex actions;
again, time constraints in transferring a 526-page
novel into a two-hour screenplay would explain
why. Still, her criticism seems justified.   As
indicated above, much of the personal motivations
for characters' actions have been deleted.   Viewers familiar with the text can interpret and
interpolate where necessary to make actions and
decisions understandable; viewers coming to the
narrative for the first time in the film might
find it more difficult. In addition, such problems as the effect Christine has on Dennis's
family and the threat she poses to Michael and
Regina Cunningham disappear entirely in the film.

     One consequence of streamlining the narrative
is that certain visual images in the film no
longer have specific referents. One of the most
intriguing performances is Roberts Blossom's
George Le Bay as the eccentric, cynical brother of
Christine's first (and until Arnie appears, only)
owner. Le Bay is a reprehensible character, foul
of speech, physically repulsive, wearing a filthy
backbrace with loose straps that flop as he walks.

     Le Bay, of course, combines two characters
from the novel. Roland Le Bay originally sells
Arnie the car; his brother George explains much of

Christine's history to Dennis after Arnie has begun to change. In the film, Blossom's character
incorporates both functions. Physically, he adds
much to the visual effect of the film; yet there
seems no inherent reason why George Le Bay should
be wearing a backbrace. In King's text, that
particular datum becomes important when we discover that Arnie, too, begins to suffer from strained
back muscles. He has literally pushed Christine
back to health, as it were. Since the film eliminates any references to Arnie pushing Christine,
and since George Le Bay has only owned the car for
a few weeks since his brother's death, the backbrace plays no functional role and becomes merely
a curious device for attracting the viewer's
attention.

At other moments, the film drops into stereotype and caricature. William Ostrander's Buddy
Repperton is physically and psychologically too
much like a later version of John Travolta's Billy
Nolan from Carrie (or even his character from
television's Welcome Back Kotter series), especially in the shop scene as he threatens Arnie.
His subsequent appearance in Darnell's garage continues that sense; curiously, when he leaps to the
top of the car and begins hammering at the
windshield, his actions parody one of Travolta's
song-and-dance numbers from Grease.

Repperton's image doesn't improve when he
suddenly finds himself in real danger. Christine
smashes into his car, and for an instant Repperton's face communicates highly realistic and
fascinating emotions--disbelief, frustration, anger, and surging fear. Then he turns and runs.

Unfortunately, in doing so he succumbs to one
of the most irritatingly hackneyed devices in the
film, one already used by Moochie Morgan. To
escape from a car, he runs down the middle of a
road.

In neither case, does the action seem un-
avoidable. Moochie was trapped shortly after
stepping out of a truck cab; apparently the truck
driver let him off in that particular spot because
it was close to where Moochie needed to go.
Equally presumably, Moochie should have been familiar enough with the area to be able to escape
Christine. Although the scene is dark, highlighted by Carpenter's signature use of bright

beams reflecting across the screen, it would seem
that Moochie could have done better than to run
down the middle of the highway or through the
driveway-areas of an industrial complex. The
death scene is fascinating as the car forces itself into a loading dock and crushes the boy. Roy
Arbogast´s special effects carry the scene, with
Christine literally ripping her fenders and sides
to pieces as she lunges into an area too narrow
for her. Arbogast says that "What you saw was
basically what really happened . . . . We weakened
the metal by acid-washing it, so it would peel
back, but the alley walls were poured concrete
that had hardened" (Kelley, "Effects Man" 56).
The overhead camera shot is highly effective, as
are the sounds of ripping metal. But all of that
is lessened by an instinctive sense that Moochie
did a foolish thing in being trapped.

Repperton´s fate is similar, and similarly
weakens an otherwise interesting special effect.
There is something powerful about the visual image
of the flaming car--a car literally from Hell--
racing through the unallayed darkness, gradually
spotlighting the fleeing figure.

On the other hand, there is something absurd
about Repperton running down the center of a
deserted road. He has already demonstrated his
abilities as a dirty street fighter, capable of
sudden and at times unexpected actions, both de-
fensive and offensive. Nor do there seem any
external reasons why he should remain on the road;
as far as we can see, the land is flat around him,
with no specific hazards that would make it even
more dangerous to leave the pavement. In the text
of course, he did precisely that, climbing over a
snowdrift in an attempt to escape Christine.
Here, he simply runs.

Again, the concluding effect is spectacular.
The flaming car strikes him and runs over him. As
Christine disappears in the distance, the camera
focuses on Repperton´s now-flaming body, an obvious visual parallel to Christine herself. Still,
there remains that uneasy afterthought: Why didn´t
Repperton act more in character and avoid the easy
stereotype.

Darnell´s death is also awkward. Carpenter
again goes for the effective visual image: Christine, smoking, hot, and ash-gray, enters the ga-

rage, sounding as if she is about to disintegrate.
Darnell follows to her stall, approaches the
ruined car, and tries to open the door. He burns
his hands, then wraps his fingers in a scrap of
cloth and pulls the door open. The inside of the
car seems as devastated as the exterior--the entire scene is gray and shadowy. Then, in a moment
that remains unexplained, he <u>sits down on the
burned-out front seat</u>. Inexplicably, he smiles,
as if pleased, setting his rifle down on the seat
beside him. At that point, he is doomed. Again,
the effect works. The radio suddenly blares (appropriately "Bony Marone") and the seat slides
forward, crushing him. But what remains a mystery
is <u>why</u> Darnell would get inside the car in the
first place. He has already seen enough to convince him that something is desperately wrong. He
knows Arnie is out of town; he knows that no one
has gotten out of the car; he knows that the car
is empty when he forces the door open; he knows
that something unimaginable is happening. So he
sits down in the car . . . and dies. Again,
visual effect overpowers inherent logic or consis-
tency.

Hogan expresses his displeasure with such
moments when he concludes that although <u>Christine</u>
is enjoyable, "it´s also an empty, gimmick-filled
movie. Neither Donald M. Morgan´s smoothly sinister photography nor the pounding rock ´n roll
score can hide the film´s triviality" (56). To a
degree he is correct.

But those elements that seem most gimmicky
can also be seen as strengths. And <u>Christine</u> is
not simply a film that failed. It does have
strengths that go far to redeem the weaknesses.

Casting works well. Keith Gordon´s Arnie
Cunningham is well handled, given the screenplay´s
abbreviated treatment of Arnie´s transformation.
Gordon is convincing as the Arnie of the film, if
not as the Arnie of King´s novel. He makes the
most of what he is given to work with, handling
all the stages of Arnie´s altering personality
with equal care. And there is an intriguing ambivalence in him, a fluctuation between naive in-
nocence and self-conscious cruelty that expresses
itself in his often-hooded eyes and sneering lips.
He expresses complex emotions without drawing explicit attention to them.

107

John Stockwell´s Dennis Guilder also captures
a character. Guilder is less important in the
film than in the novel; King´s Dennis narrates
two-thirds of the text and gives the reader most
of the critical insights into changes in Arnie and
Christine. Still, Stockwell again manages to convince in spite of the reduction in his role. He
is physically appropriate for the role, ruggedly
good-looking, not too pretty to be a football
player, not too stereotypically a "jock" to be
sensitive and caring. His self-consciousness and
diffidence places him in situations where he
clearly feels out of place: protecting Arnie
against Repperton´s threats in the school shop;
trying to convince Le Bay not to sell Arnie the
car; justifying Arnie´s actions and his own to
Regina Cunningham. He is not so fully in control
that we can expect him to handle the growing
crisis easily, yet he has the intellect and the
strength to take action when it is required. The
film´s climax loses some of its power by not
letting us see how difficult and painful it is for
Dennis to maneuver the huge machinery with his
injured leg--King´s text, told as it is from Den-
nis´s point of view, is much more convincing here;
but Stockwell creates a credible, empathetic character.

Two others characters are particularly intriguing. Blossom´s George Le Bay has already
been mentioned. In spite of contradictions in the
character, Blossom communicates just the right
cynicism, suppressed anger, and eccentricity.
Physically and psychologically, he counterbalances
the "nerdish" Arnie, with Dennis caught between
them, unable to understand the obsession of either
with Christine.

Robert Prosky is equally and appropriately
distasteful as Darnell, the acquisitive and ureth-
ical garage owner. Again, Carpenter has simpli-
fied matters greatly, glossing over many of Dar-
nell´s connections with drugs, stolen parts, and
assorted other crimes. Even so, the character
comes through clearly, providing a guideline by
which to measure changes in Arnie´s temperament as
he becomes more and more like the Le Bays and Dar-
nells of the adult world.

Harry Dean Stanton has a brief but important
role as Detective Junkins, an abbreviated version

of the more extensive (and doomed) character in
King's novel. Other characters bring substantial
acting skill to bear on the film, as in Christine
Belford's authoritarian Regina Cunningham, hiding
behind a facade of reason and democratic proced-
ures, and Robert Darnell's passively accepting
Michael Cunningham.

A second strength in the film is its visual
impact. Carpenter may be weak in his handling of
narrative and plot, but he excels in creating
specific visual images that stay with the viewer
long after the film is over. His characteristic
use of light and darkness for dramatic effect, and
his propensity for night-time shots, when the con-
trasts would be even more remarkable, had become a
trademark long before Christine, in films such as
The Fog and The Thing. In Christine, Carpenter
uses the car as focal point for a number of shots,
epitomized by the moment when Arnie stands in
front of the trashed car and says, "Show me."
Carpenter cuts from a close-up of Arnie to a shot
from behind Arnie, with boy and car barely outlined by the faint light coming through a window.
Suddenly headlights flare, narrowing to a horizon-
tal glare that bisects the frame and silhouettes
Arnie in vivid light; the accompanying sound effects increase the dramatic impact of the image
and make it one of the most memorable in the film.
Again and again, Carpenter's visual imagination
shows through as he creates scene after scene of
skillfully directed, technically flawless imagery.
For that alone, Christine would be a memorable
film.

In addition, the musical background becomes
almost as integral a part of the film as the rock
'n roll lyrics became part of the texture of
King's novel. The opening credits roll on a dark
screen, accompanied by the roaring of an automobile engine--a nerve-wracking, teeth-jarring sound
that suddenly becomes "Bad to the Bone" as the
camera cuts to an automobile assembly line in
1957. Throughout the film, Carpenter interweaves
his own electronic music (composed in association
with Alan Howarth) with period music--a dozen rock
'n roll classics selected for their appropriateness to specific scenes. For example, when Dennis
breaks into the garage shortly after Arnie has
begun work on restoring Christine and tries to

open the front door, Christine locks herself. He struggles with the handle. Suddenly, the radio blares, "Keep a knockin´ but you can´t come in."

Finally, Carpenter wisely pulls back on the more gruesome visual effects. Although there is no question as to how Moochie dies, for instance, Carpenter does not show the details in loving close-up, as he had done with violent death and gory effects in The Thing. The most extensive violence occurs when Repperton and his gang destroy Christine; otherwise, Carpenter implies rather than defines. Even Arnie´s death is more suggested than realized, with the body almost stylized in its patterns of light and shadow. Certainly the deaths of Repperton and his gang are much quicker, less lovingly described in the film than in the novel; and Darnell´s death is infinitely less painful and horrifying.

The result is a film depending more on characterization than on visual horror. Argobast commented that "For the first 45 minutes, it´s all character development. There´s no special effects at all. It really shows how John [Carpenter] has developed" (Kelley "Effects Man Argobast" 57). Characterization may be flawed, without sufficient time to demonstrate transitions from one psychological state to another, but it is far stronger than in many "monster" films, in which characters are often less important than the creatures that destroy them or the special effects that make the destruction visual. Christine does in fact invite the viewer into the frustrating world of high school adolescence, with all of its attendant fears and uncertainties, at least long enough to approach an understanding of Arnie, Dennis, and Leigh.

Carpenter also rejects King´s ghostly Le Bay. King leaves the question of the antecedent of evil open: either Christine was built inherently evil, or the evil in Roland Le Bay´s personality imbues her with ghastly powers. Carpenter places the onus directly on the car. Even before Le Bay owns her, she maims and kills. There is no explanation for the evil, but Carpenter´s Christine changes the people who own her. George Le Bay explicitly implicates Christine in the deaths of his brother, sister-in-law, and niece, and there is no question in Dennis´s mind, or Leigh´s, that Christine has

altered Arnie as well. This shift in the focus of
evil allows Carpenter to disregard the horrific
apparitions that King described so carefully, and
thus the film Christine avoids such straightforwardly horror effects as the ghosts Leigh and
Dennis see in the car during the confrontation at
Darnell's. To that extent, as with Cronenberg's
Dead Zone, Carpenter's films paradoxically defuses
the visual horror possible in the original text.
And in doing so, he strengthens the film.

Technically, filming Christine presented several difficulties, which Carpenter and his production crew admirably surmounted. By the time they
finished filming, they had located twenty-five
1958 Plymouth Furys in varying stages of decay,
restored seventeen of them, and destroyed all but
two. The stage at times resembled more a mechan-
ics bay than a film stage, as various "Christines"
were repaired and prepared for specific shots.
One car was fabricated from a special material
that looks like metal but is capable of returning
to its original shape when bent; this "Christine"
is the centerpiece of the restoration scene, as
the car shows Arnie what she is capable of:
fenders, bumpers, grills, headlights, mirrors, and
frame untwist to re-create a "pristine Christine"
after Repperton's attack.

Similarly, the spectacular explosions at the
gas station just before Repperton's death were
carefully arranged. The station was a full-scale
mock-up, so convincing that passersby frequently
stopped to fill up. Every stage of the multiple
explosions was precisely calculated--even more
carefully than usual, in light of the recent ca-
tastrophe during special-effects shooting on the
set of Landis's Twilight Zone movie. The resulting scene is startling and convincing, as wave
after wave of flames shoots into the night sky,
providing an appropriate prelude to the flaming
car and Repperton's death.

As a film Christine works. It is not fully
successful; neither is it a complete failure. One
viewer (a student in the theater department of
Pepperdine University and a staunch King fan) gave
it a C+, with perhaps an A- for effort as well.
It tried to accomplish too much. It succeeded on
some levels, faltered on others. Visually, it
excites and stimulates; in terms of narrative, it

111

assumes too much from the novel, while failing to
establish its own rationale for characters and
motives. It certainly ranks in the upper-middle
ranges of King's films--interesting, at times exciting, pleasant entertainment that neither demands too much from the viewer nor distorts King's
narrative beyond recognition.

CHAPTER X

Children of the Corn (1984)

In the September, 1985 issue of Castle Rock, King published the eighth of his "Lists That Matter," this one dealing with the worst films of all time. As number one, he listed Blood Feast, the first of the "slice-and-dice features." Numbers two through five included: Plan Nine from Outer Space, the last film featuring Bela Lugosi; Teenage Monster; Old Yeller, the "peak of sappy sentimentalism the Disney studios´ non-cartoon movies poured out until 1965"; and Chuck Norris´s Missing in Action.

Number six is Children of the Corn. "Here is another horrible movie," he says,

> and to me the most horrible thing about it is that it was based on one of my stories. Not very closely--just closely enough so the producers could call it Stephen King´s Children of the Corn, which it really wasn´t. In the movie version, the creature appears to be some sort of gopher from hell. There are some classic bad lines in this movie. "Outlander, we have your woman!" is one I like; later on the hero scooches down beside the little kid and says in a friendly voice, "Just what did this monster look like, Jobie?" . . . so far I haven´t seen any of it, and I´m not sure I want to. It might have corn-borers in it. (7)

Unfortunately, King´s assessment echoes that of almost every critic. Children of the Corn is the least effective adaptation of a King piece; and it is arguably the worst of the films when considered as a film, any relationship to Stephen King aside. It is difficult to make such a statement, if only because of the inherent strength of King´s short story, one of the most impressive in his 1978

113

Night Shift collection. The story is a 30-page examination of mystery, suspense, and horror, too short to provide enough action for a 90-minute feature film, yet in itself fully complete. In addition, to follow King's text explicitly on camera would result in a film quite possibly too intense--and certainly too unsettling--for most audiences. As finally produced, the film failed to capture either the essence or the substance of King's vision, in spite of his comment that "In some of the (King) movies, there is a trace of what I do. There's some in "Children of the Corn" (Rhetts 30).

Part of the difficulty with the film lay in the fact that production seemed to stall at every stage. In winter of 1981, King was approached about a screenplay treatment he had written for Children of the Corn. The group involved, Varied Directions, intended to film the piece with David Hoffman, best known for his work in public television, as director. As a small production company, they had difficulty funding their original project on a proposed budget of $1,000,000--too small for major investors (Wiater, "Collaboration" 29).

Two years later, the news was that Children of the Corn had recently gone into production. Paul Gagne noted that originally the film was to have been produced by Joe Masefield, directed by Harry Wiland, and financed in part through Home Box Office. When that arrangement fell through, New World Pictures stepped in and purchased rights for the project. Under the new arrangement, the film would be produced by Terry Kirby, budgeted for $3,000,000, and directed by Fritz Kiersch, whose previous credits were largely limited to directing commercials. Speaking of the budget, King said in an interview that it was low, "which isn't necessarily a bad sign, but the story is not exactly one calculated to send you out of the theater with sunshine in your heart . . . It depends on what they do with my screenplay" (Gagne, "Stephen King" 5).

What they did with King's screenplay was to alter it virtually beyond recognition, to the point that the final production gives King no screenplay credits at all. Even more to the point, it distorted the story itself, so that viewers approaching King's fiction through the film receive an irritatingly inaccurate perception of what King is trying to do. George Goldsmith revised the screenplay at least three times, with producer Donald P. Borchers instrumental in completing the final script. "Among the changes we made from the original story," Borchers comments, "was the alteration of the age and occupation of the two main protagonists." In addition, Goldsmith introduced two new characters, children disenchanted with life under the theocracy of "He Who Walks Behind the Rows." The two, Job and Sarah, were "wonderful," according to Borchers; "I then introduced two older characters in the group who believed in the religion because I wanted to see the counterpoint. And we rewrote the end, which is a total surprise because it ends in a different fashion than the original story does" (Everitt, "Children" 44). Whether the new ending was qualitatively superior to King´s remains to be seen.

From the opening scenes, it is clear that the production crew disregarded most of King´s story. The initial action takes place only three years before, rather than the thirteen of King´s story. Moving the time-frame closer to the present immediately introduced two anomalies into the film. First, there was no longer sufficient time for the cult of "He Who Walks Behind the Rows" to develop the intricacies and power the narrative requires, particularly in terms of the ritual sacrifice of children as they turned nineteen.

Second, it led to an unresolved difficulty in casting. Job, the young boy who provides much of the voice-over background at the beginning of the film, does not change materially when the film shifts to present time; yet for a child of seven or eight, a three-year lapse would cause a tremendous alteration in physical appearance. Neither, in fact, do any of the other children change from the initial slaughter in the coffee shop, although both Isaac and Malachi are present; Malachi, in fact, appears to be wearing the same clothing three years later.

This single point is merely indicative of the carelessness evident in nearly every part of Children of the Corn. Characters have little or no resemblance to King´s originals; even more frustratingly, the film seems not to have any definite narrative line, leaving King far behind

115

before the film is even half completed. Characters behave with alarming illogic, as when Malachi
viciously cuts Vicky´s cheek with his knife, presumably so that her screams will force Burt from
his hiding place; he immediately covers her mouth
with his hand, however, stifling her cries and
outshouting her with his own "Outsider, we have
your woman!" Burt and Vicky fall into stereotype
after stereotype, including the disastrous "stay
here, where it is safe" convention so frequently
abused in horror films.

Even at the level of horror itself, <u>Children
of the Corn</u> proves remarkably inconsistent. The
early attempts at inculcating fear rely entirely
on startling images, often telegraphed so early
that by the time the image actually appears, the
viewers have already stifled any reactions and
find the image itself tedious.

This is particularly damaging since director
Fritz Kiersch approached the film through a highly
stylized visual imagery. According to Borchers,
Kiersch initially envisioned as camera style in
which evil would "be seen from a sense of
height. . . . he saw the camera looking down when-
ever there was terror" (Everitt, "Children" 45).
As finally shot, the film does suggest greater
variety than just this one device; still, the visual images do not capture the viewers´ imaginations as completely as producer and director
hoped.

The first example of such a failure occurs
when Vicky approaches the boy´s body on the road.
Burt is searching in the corn; Malachi has already
circled the car with his knife drawn. The camera
follows Vicky as she walks slowly along the road,
stands over the body, kneels, and stares. At that
point, it is obvious as the camera shifts to the
covered body that something must happen; sure
enough, the boy sits up, hisses, and turns his
blood-stained face to the camera. But by that
time, the reader is already quite sure what must
occur; when it actually does, it is too little,
too late. The film then subverts even that attempt at startling by cutting immediately to Burt
shaking Vicky awake. Surprise! It was all a
dream.

The film also consistently over-uses visual
imagery. Children stand in silhouette, their

sickles and knives bared and clearly in sight;
they do this so often that they cease to be
threatening. When they do attack, as in scenes at
the roadside gas station or at Job´s and Sarah´s
old house, the sequences take so long, with so
many inter-cuttings of presumably terrifying wea-
pons gleaming through shadows, that by the time
violence erupts, it seems frustratingly superficial, quickly over and forgotten. By being so
drawn-out and so often interwoven with other
scenes intended to create dramatic tension (Burt
investigating the City Hall; Vicky being attacked
in the old house), the episodes actually defuse
their own inherent terror and become tedious, predictable, and flat.

Characters add to the sense of the overly familiar. Burt and Vicky are not the complex, difficult couple King defines. They are instead
lovers, one seeking commitment, the other rejecting it. Linda Hamilton´s Vicky sets much of the
tone for the film to follow as she steals up on
Burt (Peter Horton), innocently asleep in a motel-
room bed. The camera focuses on her feet, suggesting that since this scene follows the coffee-shop
massacre, more violence is about to explode.
Instead, she blows a party noise-maker in his ear
and wishes him Happy Birthday.

In one of two interesting cross-connections
with King, she lip- syncs "School is Out," including the lyrics King incorporated in his revised
version of "The Raft" for Skeleton Crew. Later,
as the two drive the interminable road through the
Nebraska corn, we see that she has been reading
Stephen King; a copy of Night Shift sits on the
car dashboard, providing perhaps the most ingeni-
ous moment in the film. From then on, Vicky grows
increasingly passive, eager to leave the deserted
Gatlin until she finds Sarah, then unaccountably
refusing to leave. Captured, she becomes bait for
Burt, and must be told twice to run for her life
when he finally rescues her.

Burt fares only marginally better. His reactions to the dead child on the road seem wooden,
forced upon him by the exigencies of plotting
rather than emerging from within. He refuses to
leave Gatlin, even after seeing deserted streets
with corn stalks stuffed in every trash can and
mail box. When he and Vicky are searching the

house, he manages to back into her, providing another moment of empty shock; after they discover Sarah, he suddenly leaves both of them unprotected to explore the town--the place is weird, he says, but safe, echoing the unthinking heroes of countless weak horror films. Obviously he had not read the copy of <u>Night Shift</u> on the dashboard of his car, or he would have known just how weird and how unsafe Gatlin really is.

As the film nears its climax, his character becomes even flatter. In a single cliche-ridden diatribe, he converts the assembled children from their three-year-long aberration and walks away from them unharmed--and these are the same children who slaughtered their own parents on Isaac's say-so. When he and the others huddle in the barn during the approach of "He Who Walks Behind the Rows," he suddenly takes charge, giving orders to everyone; he also seems to know each individual's name, although he hasn't had time yet to meet any of them except Job and Sarah. He discovers that the Blue Man had once tried to destroy the monster by reading the Bible; Job just happens to pull from his pocket the very page "Occifer Hotchkiss" read from three years before, with the critical verse highlighted. Fire can destroy the monster. At that moment, Burt recites my favorite "bad" line from the film, destroying any hope for other than a contrived, acceptably Hollywood ending: "Oh, yes! The gasohol!"

He leaves to confront "He Who Walks Behind the Rows," but he is safe because as he leaves, he tells Vicky, "I love you," finally making the verbal commitment he has avoided throughout the film. And having done so, he has assured his safety.

The two other main characters, John Franklin's fanatical Isaac and Courtney Gains's homocidal Malachi, offer more. Neither Franklin nor Gains is an accomplished actor; both are saddled with lines that defy natural expression, especially Isaac's pseudo-biblical prophetic utterances. Both, however, are physically appropriate for their roles. Unfortunately, they are not allowed to develop those roles as King envisioned them. Isaac is accused of being a fallen prophet, is sacrificed to "He Who Walks Behind the Rows," and returns from the dead (via a minimum of makeup) to wreak his vengeance upon Malachi.

For much of the film, Malachi must be content with frowning, yelling, brandishing his inevitable butcher knife, and clumping about in heavy boots. Finally, he rebels against both Isaac and "He Who Walks Behind the Rows," an action unthinkable in King's story. His rebellion is short-lived, serving primarily to allow Burt to rescue Vicky, who is conveniently standing at the edge of the crowd, waiting to escape. For all of his efforts, Malachi becomes an unwilling sacrifice to the god he claims to have served.

"He Who Walks Behind the Rows" is perhaps the greatest disappointment in Children of the Corn. King's story works because "He Who Walks Behind the Rows" exists, yet never appears. Unfortunately, the film tries to make visible that which cannot be made so. The result is what King describes as the "gopher from Hell"; after that image, there is little the remaining moments of the film can do to redeem it. When the corn fields finally explode in flame, "He Who Walks Behind the Rows" is represented more logically by billowing flames and finally by a pillar of fire shooting upward. Yet throughout, "He Who Walks Behind the Rows" fails to live up to either name or reputation.

There are moments when the film comes close to succeeding. The deserted streets of Gatlin are appropriately eerie, as are the corn-stalk bedecked offices in the City Hall. The scenes of the open corn fields establish a strong sense of mystery and threat, particularly for anyone who has ever felt the cutting edge of corn leaves. Even the billowing clouds and flames that herald the coming of "He Who Walks Behind the Rows" are visually acceptable.

Countering those moments, however, are too many that do not succeed. From the moment Vicky and Burt stop running and begin talking at the end of the film, it is clear that the danger is not over. Burt gets into the car, ostensibly to get their map, although the map did them little good the last time they tried to use it and Burt has already established that both Sarah and Job know how to get to Hemingford. Even as he sits down, the viewer knows what must come--and, as expected, Rachel rises from the back seat (it is not clear how she knew that Burt would survive his confron-

119

tation with the monster) and lifts her sickle, taking far more time than necessary but meeting the conventions of a startling, shocking ending.

In a way, it seems unfair--or at least ungenerous--to belabor the faults of a film such as Children of the Corn. Yet it does present a certain level of danger. King has said frequently that he does not care particularly about films made from his fiction; the original stories stand unaltered on the shelf, and no film can change a word in them. Unfortunately, there are those who judge a writer more by the films made from his words than by the words themselves. Anyone seeing Children of the Corn and assuming that the film represents King's work risks misjudging both King and the genre he enjoys most.

In any listing, some element must come last. In the case of films made from the stories and novels of Stephen King, that dubious distinction must be awarded to Children of the Corn.

CHAPTER XI

Firestarter (1984)

The film version of King's exploration of pyrokinesis was the fifth Stephen King film within
two years--or the seventh, if one includes the two
shorts, The Boogeyman and The Woman in the Room.
The film also came at a time when theaters were
flooded with horror films modeled after Carpenter's Halloween; R. H. Martin estimated that there
were some twenty-five such films released between
Halloween's appearance in 1978 and Firestarter
("Mark Lester" 14), a clear indication of the
over-kill (both figurative and literal) in horror
films that Cronenberg's Dead Zone also attempted
to avoid.

These two facts, taken together, suggest basic difficulties inherent in Firestarter: it was
inextricably associated with King's name and
reputation, in spite of the clear statements by
its producer and director that it was not a horror
film. As a King film, it followed so closely on
the heels of its predecessors--part of the notori-
ous "King Film-of-the-Month-Club" that one critic
invented--that it risked failure simply because of
King's cinematic over-exposure. Ralph Novak
closed his review of the film by arguing that
"maybe we're all King-ed out. He has become a
monster--The Horror Author Who Consumed the Pop
Culture--and we'd be better off if he'd take a
year or two off and come back as Stephen King II"
("Firestarter" 12).

Novak's comment unfairly lays blame for the
deluge of films on King, who, after all, was not
responsible for timing the release of the various
films; still, he penetrates the center of the
difficulty: with Firestarter, eleven King films
had appeared within eight years, with at least
three more feature films and two television productions imminent. The uneven quality of several
of the more recent ones, such as Christine and
Children of the Corn, coupled with the outstanding
cast assembled for Firestarter, may easily have

raised viewers´ expectations that the film could
not meet.

In addition, the nature of the novel was such
that any film made from it was bound to disappoint
a part of King´s readership. Just as did Carrie,
Cujo, and Dead Zone, Firestarter skirts the edges
of horror, at times seeming more convincingly
science fiction or even mainstream fiction. There
are no monsters in the text, no hauntings or
ghostly visitations (Collings MFSK 37-60). King´s
visual imagery is sufficient, however, to meet the
needs of his readership; even in narratives set
clearly within the possible or the plausible, he
incorporates descriptions that touch readers on
the deeper, visceral levels required to create
terror and horror.

The film attempted to do quite the opposite.
From the beginning, it divorced itself from the
classification. Producer Frank Capra, Jr., realized all along that much depended upon the audience liking and identifying with Drew Barrymore´s
Charlie McGee. Without an empathetic connection
between character and audience, the film would
disintegrate. Consequently, the film was limited
as to how much violence she could safely indulge
in; if she killed too frequently, too easily, or
too brutally, she risked alienating the viewers
who were, after all, concentrating almost all of
their attention on her plight. As a result, Capra
said, Firestarter is "not a horror picture, in the
sense that we´re not looking for scares to carry
it. It has excitement and thrills, an excellent
cast, a good story, and a very good script." It
is, he concludes, more a "fantasy adventure, perhaps . . . but it´s dealt with very realistically"
(Martin, "Oh the Set" 59).

Even so, the film was nonetheless part of the
King mystique, and that implied an expectation of
horror that simply did not materialize. Whether a
conscious decision by the production heads or not,
that single fact made it impossible for the film
to satisfy most viewers.

As with several other King properties, Firestarter also suffered from a long and tortuous development from novel to film. One of King´s most
popular novels, it was quickly optioned for film
production. Paul Gagne reports that rights first
went to an Egyptian producer, Dodi Fayed, who paid

$1,000,000 in 1980 for the opportunity of working
with the novel ("Stephen King" 5). Later, the
rights were transferred to Universal, where John
Carpenter was set to direct a screenplay by Bill
Phillips. The original screen-treatment required
a more extensive budget than Universal was willing
to support, in part because of the failure of a
number of recent horror films (again, Firestarter
suffered because of its tangential connection with
an overexposed genre), including Carpenter's The
Thing. Universal put the project on hold, and
Carpenter and Phillips went on to complete Christine instead.

It is unwise at best to speculate about what
might have happened, especially when dealing with
an art form as fluid as film. However, a few
hints suggest that the Carpenter/Phillips Firestarter might have run into even more difficulties
than the de Laurentiis version. The budget was
apparently larger than the $15,000,000 Mark Lester
had to work with. In addition, the screenplay
differed greatly from King's text, a situation
that had led to the controversies surrounding The
Shining and Children of the Corn. Phillips's
script, which R. H. Martin identifies as a revision of an even earlier treatment by Bill Lancaster for Carpenter, is said to have deleted John
Rainbird entirely, replacing that pivotal character with a woman doctor ("Mark Lester" 14).

When the Carpenter project folded, Firestarter moved yet again, this time to De Laurentiis's
production studios. Earlier scripts proved disappointing, and Stanley Mann was approached about
writing a new one. Mann's version was accepted
and actually drew praise from King. When he read
the scene in which Andy and Vicky McGee try to
"fire train" Charlie by teaching her how to toast
bread, he responded with "I wish I'd thought of
that" (Gagne, "Stephen King" 5).

De Laurentiis's choice for director, the rel-
atively unknown Mark Lester, confirmed the tone of
the film. De Laurentiis wanted a young, energetic
director who was familiar with stunts and special
effects, since Mann's script, like the novel,
would focus on Charlie McGee's pyrotechnics. Lester had directed only a few substantial films, and
those seemed of dubious value to many critics.
Novak argued, for example, that the finished film

"lacked movement":

> What should be a powerful climax, when
> Barrymore finally confronts [George C.]
> Scott, is tossed off. Maybe it would be
> wrong to expect subtlety from director
> Mark Lester, whose previous films in-
> clude Truck Stop Women. ("Firestarter"
> 12)

The titles of several of Lester´s other films in-
spire even less confidence in his ability to deal
effectively with Firestarter: Gold of the Amazon
Women, Roller Boogie and the violent Class of
1984.
R. H. Martin´s evaluation of Lester´s films
suggests a reason why de Laurentiis would have
been drawn to him. From the beginning, his work
showed a concern for social and political issues.
Twilight of the Mayans, his first film, was a documentary about exploitation, filmed in the jungles
of Mexico. Tricia´s Wedding was direct political
satire, with a female impersonator portraying
Tricia Nixon. His next film, Steel Arena, combined documentary with narrative; Martin notes
that Lester approached the film as a "documentary
of the thrill-driver´s lifestyle, while the audi-
ence--drawn in by the promise of death-defying
stunts--gets their thrills along with a tour of an
unfamiliar world." Similarly, Truck Stop Women,
which appears on one level to be an exploitative
film, works on a more sophisticated level as well.
Lester refers to a review in Rolling Stone that
"analyzed the whole political import of it, the
battle between the independent people in this
country and larger forces like the mafia." A
later film, Stunts, combined a first-rate cast
with a narrative requiring extensive use of stunt
work and effects ("Mark Lester" 12-13).
The implication in Martin´s article is that
there is indeed more to Mark Lester than one might
expect. Certainly de Laurentiis saw something of
value in his works; he spoke to Lester shortly
after viewing Class of 1984 and suggested that
they might work together. With Firestarter, the
two strands so evident in Lester´s work logically
come together: political and social commentary,
and stunts and special effects. For Lester, Fire-

starter would be a chance for a breakthrough film that would firmly establish his credibility.

Since his forte was special effects, it is not surprising that Lester agreed with Capra and Mann that Firestarter should remain true to King´s original. This was not to be an idiosyncratic film oriented toward the artistic imagery of a powerfully visual director, as was The Shining. Instead Lester followed the leads of Teague´s Cujo and Cronenberg´s Dead Zone, emphasizing relationships with King´s text rather than veering from it.

Capra agreed, stating in an interview that it had been decided to follow King´s text as closely as possible. "When you read a book," he said, "and you like what´s in the book--then why change it? . . . I think King´s readers will find every memorable and important scene included in it" (Martin "On the Set" 59).

The film does indeed respect King´s text. It is possible to watch the film with a copy of Firestarter at hand and locate almost every scene, find virtually every line of dialogue.

And, paradoxically, that leads to one of the weaknesses in the film.

There are actually two problems working in tandem against Firestarter. The first, already suggested, is that it emphasizes special effects. Most pre-release articles and previews of the film concentrated on the elaborate effects required. Mike Woods and Jeff Jarvis, who developed many of the special effects for the film, considered fear of fire the narrative "hook," the element that would engage viewers with the film (Hogan, "Firestarter" [II] 21). Consequently, special effects took over. Everything was carefully arranged; in light of the recent disaster on the Twilight Zone movie set, producer, director, and stunt coordinator worked out every eventuality in advance.

In addition, since the film´s climax included the destruction of a quarter-million dollar external mock-up of a Southern mansion, many effects could only be filmed once. Every element had to be meticulously controlled. "What is unusual about the stunts in this film," according to stunt coordinator Glenn Randall, "is that they are tremendously large in scope. . . . Everything happens to groups of people, and all at once"

125

(Hogan, "Firestarter" [I] 28).

The extreme care resulted in an accident-free production schedule and in the film´s spectacular effects. It also resulted in a "safe" film more concerned with effects than with character, motivation, or plot. Similarly, the decision that Firestarter remain true to King´s original also results in a feeling of security; other than in minor details such as the toast scene, the film takes no chances. Actors of proven ability, including Martin Sheen (brought in when scheduling difficulties made it impossible for Burt Lancaster to accept the role), come across as suppressed, their performances competent but less convincing than usual. After Sheen has been "pushed" by Andy McGee, for example, he becomes a cipher, a warm body mindlessly agreeing with anything McGee says. That sense is drawn from King´s text; but too often, it leads Sheen to stand around, hovering in the background of a scene, blank-faced and staring, without contributing to the dramatic tension.

The same problems afflict other performances. King´s Andy McGee is a difficult character who must be simultaneously active and passive, who feels a tremendous need to protect his daughter yet at the same time is physically confined, his mind clouded by drugs. At best, it would be a frustrating role to play. David Keith´s Andy, however, is forced to spend most of his time holding his temples, squinting, and bleeding at the nose. The technical problem of controlling the flow of blood was fascinating; the gelatin capsules used released "blood" only when the actor exhaled, allowing Lester more time to film the effect (Hogan, "Firestarter" [II] 24). But solving that technical difficulty did not alter the fact that Keith´s character, like most film characters afflicted with mental powers, is forced to resort to physical signals when he uses those powers. His actions seem conventional and stereotypic, particularly when the orderlies at The Shop can stop him from using mental powers by holding his hands down at his side.

Drew Barrymore´s Charlie McGee suffers even more from filmic conventions. In order to make her pyrokinesis a visible phenomenon, she must stand stock-stiff, fists clenched at her sides, hair blowing, breathing stertorious, with sweat

126

pouring from her face. In the novel, King can merely <u>assert</u> her powers; in the film, Lester must <u>show</u> them.

As a consequence, the final destruction scene becomes curiously static. Charlie McGee stares and breathes and sweats and moves zombie-like through the flames, disconcertingly detached from everything. Individually, the special effects work; but there are so many of them, and many of them so similar, that they cease to startle or amaze. In fact, after Charlie's first explosion of powers on Irv Manders's farm, the rest of the film has difficulty maintaining the tension developed there. Charlie's frequent demonstrations of her powers at The Shop become prolonged excursions into effects, culminating with ten full minutes of exploding stuntmen, exploding buildings, exploding fireballs, and assorted other pyrotechnics.

What is lost in it all is our concern for Charlie McGee as person, as child, or as victim. We are impressed by the film's special effects, rather than involved in the fates of its characters.

In a last analysis, <u>Firestarter</u> is flawed by being too obviously a "careful" movie. The script follows King's text carefully. The stunts are staged carefully (not that carelessness or blatant disregard for safety would have made a better film, of course). Characters move through their roles carefully. And the film suffers for it; it seems static, careful, and safe.

Tim Lucas includes <u>Firestarter</u> in the science fiction/fantasy volume of his series of guides to videocassettes and discs; it is not, he contends, a horror film. The film "features good supporting performances by Martin Sheen, Louise Fletcher, and Moses Gunn, but over all . . . is shapeless and unfocused. The worst Stephen King film to date" (<u>Your Movie Guide to Science Fiction</u> 37). More generous perhaps, but still critical of the film, Novak sounds disappointed as well when he says that "Despite the fact that every other minute some villain bursts into flame, this film never quite catches fire" ("<u>Firestarter</u>" 12).

While not the "worst Stephen King film to date," <u>Firestarter</u> does not live up to the movement and tension of the original. Perhaps the final scene epitomizes its failings. In King's novel, Charlie McGee arrives alone at the only place she believes will be able to tell her story to the world--the offices of <u>Rolling Stone</u> magazine. In the film, she is accompanied by the grandfatherly Irv Manders, portrayed by the comforting and reassuring Art Carney . . . and takes her story to the more conventional, more acceptable, more archetypally "safe" <u>New York Times</u>.

CHAPTER XII

Cat´s Eye (1985)

In Cat´s Eye, screenwriter Stephen King and
director Lewis Teague open up all the stops and
just have fun.

From the opening moments, as the credits
roll, King and Teague set the tone for the rest of
the film. It is semi-comic, light, entertaining,
and self-reflexive. Few viewers miss the multiple
references King makes to himself and to films of
his novels. In effect, in Cat´s Eye, King and his
works are themselves treated as "brand names,"
incorporated into the film to lend both an air of
familiarity and to let us know that neither King
nor Teague is taking himself too seriously. Cat´s
Eye does not set out to be a serious film making
an important statement; given what it does attempt, however, it succeeds.

King is present throughout the film. In the
opening shots, a Cujo look-alike, complete with
matted coat and bleary eyes, chases the eponymous
cat (variously called "Hey, you," "Sebastian," and
"General" in the three episodes) through the
streets of Wilmington, North Carolina. Director
Teague carefully recapitulates critical camera
angles from Cujo, suggesting both the sane Cujo
chasing the rabbit and the later, rabid dog
chasing Donna Trenton. In one scene, the rabbit
hides beneath an overturned boat; the visual
closure the boat´s edge provides eliminates
everything from view except the dog´s paws and
slavering muzzle, recalling Teague´s use of the
Pinto´s frame in the earlier film.

The second intrusion is equally obvious and
equally fun. Both cat and dog narrowly miss being
hit by a passing automobile--what else but a red-
and-white 1958 Plymouth Fury sporting bumper
stickers announcing "I´m Christine. I´m pure evil"
and "Rock ´n roll will never die." Just as King
increases verisimilitude and reader participation
in his novels by incorporating bits of cultural
ephemera, including brand names and allusions to

129

popular culture, so his screenplay integrates his own career into Cat's Eye.

Nor is that the only reference. As James Wood's Morrison settles back with a drink, his television plays the critical "Would you kill Hitler" scene from Dead Zone, nicely touching upon three of the four films released during the preceding year; the presence of Drew Barrymore is sufficient to suggest Firestarter. But King is not satisfied merely to assert his presence as cultural phenomenon. When Morrison spills his drink, he stalks angrily away, complaining that he can't make sense out of the film and he doesn't know "who writes this crap anyway!" Given King's reputation and readership, if Morrison truly doesn't know, he must be one of the few holdouts in the country.

A more peripheral reference to King occurs in the name of the private school Morrison's daughter attends: Saint Stephen's School for the Exceptional.

In the second episode, as Robert Hays's Norris threatens Kenneth McMillan's Cressner, the older man fingers a copy of Penthouse on a table. Although not the July 1976 issue, the magazine does remind us where "The Ledge" was first published.

Later, in the third episode, Hugh and his wife are reading in bed. Although he closes his book too quickly to show the title, she is reading Pet Sematary and should, by all rights, be more attuned to her daughter's plight than she seems.

King's "presence" in the film highlights other allusions as well. As in Christine (both novel and film), musical accompaniment provides comic counterpoint to action. When the cat is placed in the electrified cage, it jumps to the rhythms of "Twist and Shout." Morrison's smoker's nightmare at the party features "Every Step You Take, I'll be Watchin' You." His wife's torment is accompanied by "Too Many Teardrops."

In addition, Cat's Eye refers to other films, and not always the ones we might expect. The pigeon in "The Ledge" suggests Hitchcock's The Birds on a smaller and (given Norris's treatment of it) more comic level. Cressner alludes to The Girl, The Gold Watch, and Everything as well as to Mary Poppins: "Well begun is half done."

130

Yet another allusion occurs when Morrison hands his daughter a new doll. The doll, complete with brown yarn hair and adoption papers, is named Norma Jean--a parody of Marilyn Monroe.

Taken together, these elements neatly defuse any sense of horror that might linger after the opening credits--and to justify King's first and as yet only PG-13 rating on a feature film. Cat's Eye does not claim to be a serious or terrifying show, as so many of the others did. Instead, it simply shows King doing as screenwriter what he does best in print: telling stories.

There is, of course, a structure to support the three tales. As with Creepshow, Cat's Eye is an anthology piece with three loosely linked episodes. The narrative connections are weaker than in the earlier film; Drew Barrymore appears in various guises to the cat and urges him to hurry, to rescue her. At first--and indeed until well into the third episode--we have few clues as to the problem. The links do not provide sufficient information to engage the viewer, which allows us to concentrate attention on the segments themselves.

In another sense, however, the film tries to fit together. In the beginning, the cat is in Wilmington, North Carolina; it finally escapes the Cujo clone by jumping into a Wilmington tobacco company truck, which deposits it in New York City. "The Ledge" takes place in Atlantic City, and in "The General," the cat arrives full circle, returning to Wilmington. It is a neat little device, but not strong enough by itself to give the film coherence.

More importantly, each episode builds on the preceding. "Quitters, Inc." is played largely for comic effect, in spite of the underlying current of threat. Alan King's mafioso-style Donati provides a nice foil to Wood's naive and disbelieving Morrison. Donati's strong-arm man, Junk, is physically imposing . . . but unfortunately for his reputation is given to such horrific expletives as "Oh, fiddledysticks" and "Oh, darn." In a moment of panic, Morrison almost beats his golf clubs to death, then tosses his umbrella-weapon into the closet . . . and hears a resounding "oooph" from the hidden watcher. The party scene quickly degenerates into a smoker's nightmare, in which

even the potato salad develops eyes and watches
Morrison for any signs of weakness. Regardless of
any subliminal appeals for sympathy, the episode
continually undercuts itself, forcing the viewer
to laugh instead of wince.

The second episode lightens the comic touch
considerably. "The Ledge" opens with the cat
threatened on a busy street, the object of a bet
as to whether or not it will cross safely. And
certainly the decapitation at the end would be inconsistent with the tone of "Quitters, Inc"; the
threats are more evident and more immediate, visually represented. The episode follows closely
King's tone in the original story from Night
Shift; "Quitters, Inc.," on the other hand, has
been treated more as burlesque. The camera work
accentuates Norris's danger, just as Kenneth Mc-
Millan communicates Cressner's possessiveness and
madness; unlike Leslie Nielsen in the parallel
role in Creepshow, McMillan relies less on camp
than on realistic responses tinged with craziness.

Elements of comedy survive, nonetheless, in
such overt forms as Cressner's strong-arm man,
Ducky, and his absurd T-shirt. Cressner's repeated attacks on Norris each have a slightly hysterical quality, particular when he blasts an
airhorn in Norris's face. Norris loses his balance and falls, followed by the airhorn. As the
horn plummets, the camera follows it, creating a
parodic reflection of the falling helicopter in
Superman I. More importantly, the airhorn is actually a set-up for the final comic motif. Forced
to walk the ledge himself, Cressner encounters the
ubiquitous pigeon. He kicks at it and, in an episode not found in the original story, falls. As
he in turn plummets, we see a close-up of the
cat's eyes . . . and hear a comically truncated
blast from the trumpet, merging into a thick
squish as Cressner hits it. During Cat's Eye's
theater run, audiences frequently laughed at the
moment.

With the third episode, "The General," the
comic touches lighten even further. Here we again
see a visible threat, but now it is a child--a
little girl--who is threatened, and the danger
comes from a supernatural source invisible to the
adults who should protect her. King and Teague
again do much to defuse outright horror. Scenes

of the cat hunting and killing a bird are intercut
with the ritual chases in Tom and Jerry cartoons.
The mother warns Amanda against keeping the cat in
the bedroom at night, citing Sylvester and
Tweetie-Bird as moral exempla; the troll's first
act is to shinny up the bird-cage stand, much as
Sylvester constantly tries to do, and attack Pol-
ly. Here, however, the cartoon analogy breaks down
as the Troll kills the bird.

The troll acts as the centerpiece of the episode and hence of Cat's Eye. He is the danger the
ghostly Amanda has warned the cat of from the beginning; through the craft of Carlo Rambaldi, he
is particularly appropriate: ugly and gruesome
enough to be frightening, with rows of piranha-
sharp teeth, glowing red eyes, and a knife that
gleams menacingly. At the same time, however, his
facial expressions and constant mumbling become,
if not endearing, at least non-threatening. He is
obviously dangerous, as we understand when he
steals Amanda's breath; on the other hand, he is
so equally obviously comical in his various escape
ploys when the cat finally comes to the rescue,
that it seems quite appropriate for Amanda to say
he was "played" to death on her record player.
The Troll succeeds in appealing to opposing emotions: he frightens (although does not terrify or
horrify) and he makes us laugh.

That is the leitmotif King and Teague weave
into the film from beginning to end. Cat's Eye is
not a typical King production--or at least, it
seems atypical to those accustomed to seeing The
Shining, Salem's Lot, and Cujo; or to reading most
of King's novels. But King is not an uncompromis-
ingly serious writer. "The Lonesome Death of Jordy Verrill," and even more explicitly his early
comic-satiric western "Slade" (cf. SWSK 17-22),
demonstrate King's sometimes macabre sense of humor. In Cat's Eye, he gives that humor free rein,
and the result is entertaining and engaging.

Cat's Eye was not a box-office hit. In fact,
King has compared it to Creepshow:

> At this point, I've had two screenplays
> produced and actually brought out. One
> was Creepshow, which was a good-sized
> success, and the second was Cat's Eye,
> which, financially speaking, was a good-

sized failure. (Herndon, "New Adventures" 7A)

The reason for the film's weak showing, King
continues, was primarily that MGM underwent an
executive shake-up at about the time Cat's Eye was
released. Pictures produced under the direction
of executives involved in the changes were suddenly without backers; "there were no trailers, no
publicity, no promotion--that sort of thing." In
addition, King recognized the inherent dangers of
the anthology format. In an interview with Stanley Wiater and Roger Anker in the March, 1985 issue of Fangoria, he argued that Cat's Eye was not
in fact an anthology piece. "The story of the cat
works in it, " he said, "so actually it becomes
like a maligned Disney picture. And you're not
even aware there's a number of episodes going on
so much as you are whether or not the cat's going
to save the little girl at the end and not get run
over by the truck or eaten by the dog" (12). By
the time of the Herndon interview, he admitted
that both Creepshow and Cat's Eye were anthology
movies; "It'll be interesting to see what happens
with Silver Bullet," he continues, "which is actually a 'movie' movie" (7A).
Reactions to the film varied, of course, but
were generally more consistent and more favorable
than responses to such films as Children of the
Corn.
Lawrence French refers to the film as an
"ill-conceived DeLaurentiis [sic] production," in
which King "allowed Mr. DeLaurentiis to convince
him to try and unify the three stories by having a
cat appear in all of the segments." Comedy and
terror never quite balance, primarily because the
cat's intrusion into scenes disturbs both the
dramatic tension and the continuity of humor;
French does, however, approve of the final confrontation between the cat and the troll, the
latter having a "personality that alternates from
Ewok-type cuteness, to the mischievousness nature
of Joe Dante's GREMLINS." On the whole, however,
he says in conclusion, Cat's Eye disappoints rather than entertains.
Julie Salamon's Wall Street Journal review
takes a more moderate approach. Most films based
the "nutso weirdness" in King's stories "metamor-

134

phose into clumsy and unscary cinema"; the four
King films released in the preceding eighteen
months, she concludes, were "clunkers." Not so
Cat's Eye, which "is a hoot even if it isn't exactly spine-tingling." Salamon prefers the first
episode, with the second too dependent upon a gimmicky ending, and the third the weakest of all.
The troll, however, is "a deliciously vile creation."

Coming from the opposite perspective, Gahan
Wilson considered Cat's Eye the best of the summer
films for 1985, slightly better than Ladyhawke and
far superior to Baby, Secret of the Lost Legend.
Cat's Eye is "so much better than [King's] previous anthology film, Creepshow, that it's mind-
boggling," Wilson argues, suggesting that King may
now have hit his stride in working with films.
Again, he finds the first scene most powerful ("if
the others had been up to it, I think the film
would be a sort of legend"); the second "plenty
cute" if fairly standard; and the third in need
of some revision but still satisfactory. For Wilson, the cat works well as a narrative link; he
even notes explicitly that the device was "a con-
cept of none other than Dino di Laurentiis [sic]
himself." The film as a whole "adds up to excellent entertainment," promising more and better
things from King (96-97).

In assessing the three critiques, it seems
that the truth lies somewhere between Salamon and
Wilson. Cat's Eye is an entertaining film. It
holds together perhaps more fully than French
gives it credit for, although viewers are often
less concerned with how the cat will rescue the
girl than mystified as to what is going on. Only
with the third segment is there a clear connection
between the anthology frame and the individual
stories. In addition, while the film is capable
of both subtle and broad humor and generally moves
well, there are still odd moments when it seems
drawn out, when the comedy does not pick up the
proper beat.

Cat's Eye does indicate several degrees of
improvement over Creepshow; and it does argue for
King's increasing sense of ease in working with
film. As a film, it succeeds moderately. As a
promise of things to come--Silver Bullet, Overdrive, Pet Sematary--it is far more exciting and

135

satisfying. In it we see King giving cinematic
shape to his own words and ideas.   In   spite of
King's hand in writing the   screenplay, <u>Creepshow</u>
remained largely a pastiche of E. C. comics given
visual representation by the directorial   imagination of George A. Romero. As with <u>Creepshow</u>, King
originally intended to act in the film--a cameo
role as the animal shelter   attendant;   scheduling
demands did not allow him to be present on the day
the scene was shot, however.   In <u>Cat's Eye</u>, on the
other hand,   King's   contributions   are   more
immediate and more apparent in the tone of characterization and narrative than in his physical
presence. And the film is stronger for that,

CHAPTER XIII

Silver Bullet (1985)[1]

Silver Bullet is not Cycle of the Werewolf.
And that is perhaps for the best. The
changes from one to the other make for a tighter
film. As happens often with novel-into-film (or
in this case, novella-into-film, an even more difficult proposition since the filmmakers have to
add material to reach the necessary length), there
have been a number of alterations as Cycle of the
Werewolf underwent several revisions as a screenplay. As happens less frequently, however, the
changes help the film, making it in some ways more
satisfying than the original.

First, the calendar-format has disappeared.
What made Cycle so powerful--the inexorable march
of events over months, beginning and ending with a
new year--has been lost. In its place, King sub-
stitutes a narrower time frame: beginning of summer vacation through Halloween night. This leads
to a number of subsidiary changes: the deaths come
much faster, with most of the attacks occuring
during the first half of the film; the canceled
fireworks become secondary, since they are simply
part of an October festival (itself canceled), rather than the Fourth of July; and Marty's letters
to Reverend Lowe are mailed only a day apart.
Things move faster. The monthly vignettes disap-
pear--along with the sense inherent in Cycle of
random selection of victims. Lowe makes it clear
in one scene, for example, that Stella Randolph
dies because she was about to commit suicide--a
mortal sin in the eyes of the church. Rather than
the image of a love-sick, overweight, isolated romantic, as in Cycle, we have a young woman (overweight but attractive enough to have gotten preg-
nant out of wedlock) killed in the act of taking
her own life. As Lowe boasts, he destroyed her
physical body but saved her soul.

The second change is equally critical. Cycle
does not introduce Marty Coslaw until mid-year.

Even then the boy disappears for several months as the isolated vignettes continue, although King's "Foreword" to the omnibus edition of Cycle and the original Silver Bullet screenplay indicates that he was aware almost immediately of how important the boy was to the narrative:

> . . . I started to write about this kid named Marty, who was stuck in a wheelchair, and how burned he was because the werewolf had not been content with just killing people; now the werewolf had managed to get the big Fourth of July fireworks show cancelled.
>
> The installment spilled far over the arbitrary five-hundred word limit I had imposed on myself, but I didn't care. I was excited, almost feverish. (11-12)

Silver Bullet reverses the effect of Marty's late appearance in Cycle and concentrates on him almost from the beginning. The film opens with the first death--Arnie Westrum murdered while working on the railroad tracks. It then shifts immediately to a picnic in Tarker's Mills, with a voice-over by Tovah Feldshuh as the mature Jane Coslaw. The device suggests the voice-over in To Kill a Mockingbird, even down to the timbre of the voice and the sense of nostalgia for a critical event that altered the characters' lives, regardless of how dangerous or frightening it was at the time. Almost simultaneously, the film introduces Jane, her crippled brother Marty, and the Reverend Lester Lowe. From the beginning, it concentrates on the central characters.

By altering his attention from werewolf to the Coslaws and their intricate family relationships, King provides a more coherent story-line for Silver Bullet than was evident in the admittedly episodic Cycle of the Werewolf. Marty's often superficially antagonistic, always loving relationship with his sister (who has a much amplified role in the film) parallels the equally antagonistic yet loving sibling relationship between their mother and Uncle Red. Marty's physical handicap parallels Uncle Red's emotional and psychological handicap. Jane and her mother must both discover how best to protect their brothers, while allowing them to stand on their own and preserve their own independence. The cross-generational tensions give Silver Bullet an intriguing psychological depth.

King's screenplay also alters relationships, however. Marty's father has a smaller role in the film; the sense of an inordinately physical man embarrassed by his crippled son and incapable of expressing any true emotion is lost, to the detriment of that character. In the film, the father is important only because he drives the family station wagon and carries groceries. Even though the mother is more central to the narrative, she too remains flat, a paradigmatic parent, most likely unwilling to believe her son's story and easily manipulated out of the house on Halloween by Red's stratagem.

Uncle Red is as important in Silver Bullet as Uncle Al in Cycle, if not more so. His character is far more complex in Silver Bullet. He is a drinker verging on drunkard; he is in the process of his third divorce, an act which his sister cannot understand or forgive. He plays poker for baseball cards with Marty, swearing and cursing in front of the boy and his mother. But he loves Marty--the film implies that that love goes deeper than any other Red has experienced, since he devotes hours to building a souped-up wheelchair for Marty. That chair, the Silver Bullet, saves the boy's life. And finally, while Uncle Red only partially believes Marty and Jane and their story of a werewolf, he does believe sufficiently to have the silver bullet made (cinematically one of the most impressive episodes in the film, by the way), to arrange for the parents to be gone, and to sit up with the children on Halloween. At the last moment, his rationalism reasserts itself and he removes the silver bullet from the gun. Just then, of course, the werewolf attacks. Unlike Cycle, Silver Bullet gives Uncle Red a far more active role. He fights the werewolf while Marty and Jane struggle to replace the bullet and fire the fatal shot. In most ways, then, Uncle Red's characterization in the film surpasses that in the novella; Gary Busey's acting opens the character even more, convincing the audience of the depth of his love for Marty.

139

The sister, Jane, has also changed. As noted already, she provides the opening and closing voice-over. Beyond connecting with the power of To Kill a Mockingbird, the voice-over also reassures the viewer that the main characters will survive, something that Cycle did not do explicitly. Her mature voice and the past-tense verbs make it clear to viewers that the experiences of the summer alter her and Marty as much for good as for evil. At the same time, the film establishes in its opening scenes the deep and complex relationship between Jane and her brother. Rather than merely being given to occasional sniping remarks about his being crippled, she is allowed a full range of reactions, from frustration to anger to childish petulance to deep love and trust. Jane is the first to hear about Marty´s encounter with the werewolf; she tracks down the man with an injured eye the next day; she gives Uncle Red her crucifix to be melted down with Marty´s medallion to make the silver bullet; she mails the letters to Lowe; and she stays with Marty and Uncle Red, battling the monster physically to give Marty enough time to retrieve the bullet.

Where Cycle emphasizes divisiveness and isolation, Silver Bullet concentrates on unity and love and trust--but only on a limited scale. After the violence of the first episodes, Tarker´s Mill becomes a ghost town. People huddle in their homes, distrusting and fearful. The streets are empty, stores closed, individuals afraid to talk to neighbors. Even Marty´s parents reflect that fear. But Marty and Jane draw closer, then bring Uncle Red into the tightness of their trust. For that reason, it is appropriate that the film end with the three of them together, safe at last.

Given the changes in characterization for the Coslaws, it is not surprising that the werewolf also undergoes essential alterations. Everitt McGill is perfectly cast, even for viewers who have Cycle clearly in mind. He is tall, gaunt, dark in a handsomely threatening way. Physically, he fits the role. Unfortunately, the film Lowe is fully aware of who he is and what he is, to the point that he overtly threatens both Jane and Marty (resulting in an almost requisite chase scene). The sense of Reverend Lowe as caught in something he cannot understand has disappeared;

instead, he knows from the beginning who is sending the letters and whom he must kill at the next full moon when the wolf-part has complete control.

As a result, the supernatural elements seem flatter in the film than in the novel. The transformation scene during Lowe´s funeral sermon for three victims works well but seems brief. On the other hand, his own transformation to and from werewolf adds nothing--either thematically or visually--to the existing body of werewolf lore and imagery. When he becomes the werewolf, the monster seems too much a man in a rubber suit, especially after the kinds of visual imagery created in An American Werewolf in London. In addition, the film shows the monster (or parts of it--hairy hands, elongated feet, glowing red eyes, perhaps just an inexplicable footprint) quite early, eliminating any inherent tension as to who or what is doing the killing; in spite of Steve Dimeo´s criticism that Silver Bullet "falls into the vicious cycle of most werewolf cliches, relying for suspense on the painfully predictable identity of the monster behind all the killings" (43), there is in fact no such tension in the film. Marty´s twin discoveries that there is a werewolf and that Jane and Uncle Red believe him are dramatically far more important.

The fact of a werewolf is also simply asserted without explanation or discussion. While that worked in the novella, it is less effective here. Again, Dimeo faults the film for failing to provide some rationale for Lowe´s transformation, and with some justification. In Cycle of the Werewolf King was able to enter into Lowe´s mind and reveal that there was in fact no rationale, just as there was no obvious rationale for Marty´s handicaps, or for the moral and physical handicaps of the werewolf´s many victims (cf. Collings MFSK 82-83). In Silver Bullet, such background is impossible, resulting in a film that at times threatens either pretentiousness or boredom as it works through the conventions of werewolf lore.

What helps it avoid either is the screenplay itself. Personal interchanges are more complex and more satisfying. After the vivid death of Arnie Westrum in the opening scenes, the films modulates gradually into a less gory film than one might expect. Stella Randolph´s death is visual

and graphic, perhaps unnecessarily so. The third
death more resembles Deke´s in King´s "The Raft"
than anything, with the victim pulled through the
splintered floor of a greenhouse--but the viewer
sees even less of the werewolf. In the careful use
of light and shadows, silence, and camera angles,
director Daniel Attias creates one of the tensest
moments in the film. What is potentially the most
distressing death-scene of all--the boy with the
kite--is handled through indirection and suggestion. The sheriff´s response to finding the
bloody "Happy Face" kite may be the most unnerving
in the entire film. Nor do we see any graphic
representation of death. Brady´s father kneels
over the body; we see only the father´s head and
upper torso lit from beneath by a ghastly red
glare than communicates blood without showing it.

Additionally, the film retains a number of
King´s distinctive verbal plays. The humor underlying much of the film disturbed a number of viewers; to cite Dimeo again, the film´s "graphic
viciousness, like most horror films lately, is not
only ploddingly gratuitous, but often unintention-
ally ludicrous." Dimeo sees the "Peacemaker" episodes, for example, as illustrating the failed
irony that mars the film; what he apparently
misses is the continuing thread of dark humor that
has characterized King´s screenplays, from Creepshow to Cat´s Eye to Silver Bullet.

In the original script, the horror of West-
rum´s death is offset by wild humor as the werewolf first steals a drink of Westrum´s beer,
then--after disposing of Arnie--rummages around in
his things, finds and drinks another bottle of
beer to the accompaniment of the Reingold beer
jingle sung in its "gutteral [sic] . . . subhuman"
voice, and finally tries to eat the bottle itself
(King, Silver Bullet 143-144). The effect of the
scene as written is uncomfortably and almost un-
bearably funny, a foretaste of things to come. It
seems unfortunate that it was cut from the final
film.

That macabre humor persists throughout Silver
Bullet. Almost the first words spoken in the film
are, in fact, "The boogeyman," an off-hand reference to another King story, very much on a par
with the extra-textual allusions to stories and
novels in the opening shots of Cat´s Eye. Uncle

Red´s comic reference to The Hardy Boys Meet the Werewolf works at the same level. King´s "brand name" technique emerges occasionally, as when Jane notes that she can buy ´Leggs at the local pharmacy for $1.49, or when a particular brand of liquor sits in full view on Uncle Red´s night-table. When one character turns to another during the night-time hunt for the beast and accuses him of making "lemonade in your pants," we know that no one but King could have written that line.

Even at the moments of highest tension (or perhaps particularly at those moments), the film indulges in mild humor. A double-snapping bear trap breaks the tension at just the right moment (and probably breaks the character´s ankle). The "Peacemaker" baseball bat changes hands at a critical moment, suddenly emerging from the fog from the wrong side of the screen, now wielded by an oddly shaped, dark, hairy arm; the scene suggests a wildly inappropriate parody of Kubrick´s 2001.

On the other hand, there are moments when the screenplay does not work as well. Several characters spend too much time talking to themselves, repeating the same lines with little or no variation. The third victim, Milt Sturmfuller, has trouble stringing more than three words together without using an obscenity. He deflates much of the tension preceding his death by continually spouting threats. When he finally shuts up and allows the silence to work on him (and on the audience) as he enters the spooky greenhouse where we know the werewolf lurks, the scene improves.

Other episodes telegraph events too overtly. When Uncle Red hands Marty a fireworks-rocket and makes a point of telling him to fire it last, we know how that rocket will be used. Most of the deaths are obvious long before they actually happen--the purpose of Silver Bullet was not to frighten as much as to generate momentary shocks when the creature suddenly springs, accompanied by conventional musical themes (i.e., the violins from Psycho) that tell viewers they should be frightened.

This particular flaw develops flagrantly in the final scene, an echo of De Palma´s equally weak ending shock from Carrie. Defying all internal logic in the film, the presumably dead Lowe recapitulates the werewolf while in human form, all for the sake of a last-moment scare. King apparently thought carefully about including this particular "shocker" in the film. The original screenplay indicates that Marty shoots. The silver bullet strikes the creature's remaining good eye, blinding it; it is "half WEREWOLF and half LOWE. . . . It BELLOWS again, convulses . . . and dies" (253).

Marty has a brief line of dialogue, then the scene continues:

> Here's a creature that is mostly FATHER LOWE collapsed in the remains of MARTY'S wheelchair; beyond it, MARTY is lying on the floor. UNCLE AL goes by the corpse. JANE starts by . . . and LOWE sits bolt upright for a moment, grasping blindly at her.
>
> She shrieks and darts aside. LOWE falls back, now really dead. I think. Until the sequel. (254)

The reference to "Uncle Al" identifies the screenplay as an early version, written before he became Uncle Red. And it specifies that the fallen creature is mostly Lowe; if there is in fact still a bit of the werewolf inherent in Lowe's corpse, there would be some justification for the grasping lunge a few seconds later. As filmed, however, it is clear that the corpse is entirely Lowe. As in all good werewolf films, the creature has changed back upon its death to the human form it once inhabited. For the body to then sit up and grab at Jane seems far less acceptable.

In spite of such falterings, the film does work. It concentrates on themes and motifs familiar to King's readers as well as to viewers of many contemporary horror films: isolation, fear, trust and mistrust, and children versus adults. Uncle Red is presented as an overgrown child, incapable of forming a lasting, mature relationship but capable of helping Marty and Jane in their crisis; the parents disappear, leaving the children to handle their own problems.

Silver Bullet is not a great movie, even within the narrow confines of the werewolf genre; nor is it a bad one. If there is any single ques-

tion the film raises, it might be simply "Why?"
Why yet another werewolf film?

It is clear from King's prose that he generally feels no particular affinity for the werewolf
as either tradition or character. With two exceptions, he prefers alternative monsters: ghosts,
vampires, amorphous blobs, etc. Wolf, the werewolf in The Talisman is treated with touching
depth, but it is clear that he comes to this frame
from the Territories; he is not at all the same
kind of creature as the Reverend Lowe. In those
differences--including his propensity for wearing
Oshkosh bib-overalls--rests Wolf's appeal for King
and for his readers. It is almost unfair to clas-
sify him as part of the standard horror tradition.

In IT, King also incorporates a werewolf, but
as with so much in that novel, the figure is again
not the stereotypical werewolf we might be tempted
to associate with "the master of horror." Instead
IT's werewolf is a direct reflection of film, important not as a werewolf but as a guise assumed
by It in It's continuing battle with the seven
children and their adult counterparts. It might
even be argued that there is indeed no werewolf in
the novel at all; along with all of the other monsters, it is only one manifestation of a more
frightening entity--It.

Perhaps because King really is not interested
in the werewolf as image, Silver Bullet adds little to the existing mythology, explores few areas
not otherwise explored, elicits neither true terror nor lasting fear. It disregards the unusual
suggestions King makes in Cycle of the Werewolf
concerning the hows and why of lycanthropy. Nor
does it acknowledge the difficulty of treating the
werewolf theme conventionally after such innovative films as An American Werewolf in London.
Dimeo concludes that the film "opts . . . for
showy superficiality, shunning the visual inven-
tiveness, say, of Wolfen (1981), the witty self-
mockery of The Howling (1981), or the psychological depth of the classic that started it all, The
Wolf Man (1941)." It also avoids the soft-core
pornographic sensuality of The Howling II or the
self-directed parody of Teen Wolf, which in some
ways seems the only viable form that werewolf
films can presently take. We no longer take them
seriously; all that remains is for us to laugh at

them.

As werewolf film, <u>Silver Bullet</u> is curiously old-fashioned, almost nostalgic. It concentrates more on character than on special effects. Carlo Rambaldi's often obligatory-seeming transformation scenes build upon those in recent films, without adding much new. Perhaps Dimeo is in part correct when he says that the film shows no "ambition"; it seems content to fit into the comfortable niche of werewolf film.

It entertains; it tries for little more. Still, it is among the better translations of King's prose into film, with neither the directorial idiosyncracies of Kubrick's <u>The Shining</u> nor the narrative excrescences of <u>Children of the Corn</u>. It shows more humor than Lester's pretentiously static <u>Firestarter</u>, even if it lacks the moody, brooding presence of Cronenberg's <u>Dead Zone</u>. And it develops characters with depth and humanity. Watching Marty as he in turn watches his friends running and playing baseball more than makes up for the superficial elements that occasionally intrude. Listening to the mature Jane as she reminisces about that fateful summer generates responses in areas that have little to do with fear and terror, and even less with horror. And in those episodes, <u>Silver Bullet</u> succeeds completely.

All in all, an enjoyable film.

NOTES

[1]A shorter version of this chapter appeared as "<u>Silver Bullet</u>: Another Opinion" in <u>Castle Rock</u> (December 1985).

CHAPTER XIV

Short Features:
"The Word Processor of the Gods" (1984);
"The Boogeyman" (1982),
"The Woman in the Room" (1983);
and "Gramma" (1986)

During the past two years, four Stephen King
stories have been produced as other than feature-
length films. Two were included as episodes on
television anthologies series: "The Word Processor
of the Gods" for Laurel Productions´s Tales from
the Darkside (November 1984); and "Gramma" for
Twilight Zone (February 1986). Two other film
productions have been distributed on videocasette:
"The Boogeyman" and "The Woman in the Room."

1. "The Word Processor of the Gods"

Of all the film versions of King´s material,
the most difficult to work with is the Tales from
the Darkside episode, "The Word Processor of the
Gods." It has not been released as a videocasette, and as a segment of a new series televised
in 1984/85, it did not receive as much publicity
as one might have expected. As a result, I was
unable to watch this entry in the "Stephen King
Film" sweepstakes. That is unfortunate, since the
information about the film makes it sound particularly appealing.
"The Word Processor of the Gods" is a dis-
tinctively filmable piece. Originally published
as "The Word Processor" in Playboy (1983) and reprinted under the amplified title in Skeleton
Crew, the story is unusual for King. With "The
Reach" and the soon-to-be-published IT, "The Word
Processor" is one of the few narratives which end
optimistically. It is a curiously gentle piece,
with an empathetic central character surrounded by
an unloving wife and son, frustrated by memories
of his true love stolen (as is typical in King´s
fictions) by an older brother. Through the mediation of the word processor, Richard Hagstrom re-

147

stores justice to an unjust world, and brings order out of chaos and love out of hatred and indifference. The story is lighter in effect than "The Reach" and much lighter than the massive IT, yet parallels both narratives in tone and effect.

Bringing it to television seemed a natural. The story is limited in cast and setting, with a mimimum of special effects. Most of the important changes in the narrative are internal, as Richard Hagstrom discovers the power to make his life what he wants it to be. And there are no nasty surprises; in the story, wishing makes it so, through the "Execute" and "Delete" keys on the word processor given Hagstrom by his dead nephew.

In the capable hands of Michael McDowell, the narrative could translate well into film. McDowell has demonstrated his skill in his six-volume Blackwater series, and worked on three other episodes for Tales from the Darkside in addition to "The Word processor." Director Michael Gornick had been affiliated with Creepshow as director of photography and thus would be conversant with King and King's fictions; his work with other Romero films, including Martin, Dawn of the Dead, Knightriders (in which King had a small role), and Day of the Dead, also indicates his involvement with the genre.

2. "The Woman in the Room" and "The Boogeyman"

Much more can be said about the next two films, Frank Darabont's "The Woman in the Room" and Jeff Schiro's "The Boogeyman." Both films run approximately half an hour; both are independent films, with all the difficulties such films entail. To make the matter even more complicated, they were originally released with a third, non-King film by Native Sons International, in an arrangement that led to the cassettes being removed from store shelves; only recently has Granite Films officially released the two King films as the Stephen King Night Shift Collection.[1]

The films are radically uneven in quality. The Boogeyman is by far the least successful. The film is grainy, the sound distorted; the background music is traditional "creepy movie" music, with sufficient clues to defuse any suspense.

The acting is adequate, although Lester Billings comes off as almost insane far too soon,
even before the opening credits run and he finds
his son's body in the bathtub (a weak borrowing
from <u>Psycho</u> and the pull-back-the-curtain-but-
there's-no-body-until-you-look-down films. The
psychiatrist, Dr. Harper, doesn't enter the film
until midway through; in the beginning, the film
introduces a nosy neighbor and a police investiga-
tor who virtually accuses Billings of child abuse
(the previous death had occurred only a few months
before). All of that is terribly misleading, moving the film away from the supernatural and into
rather typical crime drama. Wayne Sallee comments
that in most of the film, Billings comes across as
a "poster adult for Parents Who Beat Their Children. Kubrick did the same in <u>The Shining</u>; the
only difference in the two films is that it worked
for Kubrick" (2).

Finally, however, Billings goes to the psychiatrist and begins telling the story. Flashbacks, nicely edited to blend with Billings on the
doctor's couch, tell most of the story. From
there the film picks up speed. It handles the
threatening closet door well, with rapid cuts of
doors and knobs, shadows, lights, and mist seeping
underneath the doors. It also avoids showing the
boogeyman himself--or much of him. The last
scene, where Billings confronts his own fear,
works well cinematographically, although, as Sallee notes, the nature of the Boogeyman has been
altered far too much.

<u>The Woman in the Room</u>, on the other hand, is
superb. Sallee unfairly passes over the film with
the brief comment that since the audio was missing
on the cassette he watched, he could not review
it: "The picture was terrible, too, that should
have given me an idea as to what travesties were
to come," even though he admits to not having actually watched "The Woman in the Room."

In fact, "The Woman in the Room" may be among
the best film representations of a King narrative.

As is usual with adaptations, the screenwriter, Frank Darabont (who also directed) altered
King's original text. Instead of having Johnny
meet with doctors to discuss his mother's case,
Darabont makes him a lawyer and includes a meeting

149

with a client, a convicted multiple murderer. The
confrontation between the two men in a stark prison room neatly parallels Johnny´s visits to his
mother--in both cases, he is obsessed with death
. . . with murder. The prisoner, played by Brian
Libby, is an ex-Vietnam vet (Anthony Magistrale,
who wrote about "Children of the Corn" as a Vietnam allegory, might appreciate that bit of contemporary social commentary). He is also a professional killer, who refuses to plead insanity to
save his life. He is a professional ("A PROFES-
SIONAL!," he yells at one point) and does what he
does efficiently and without any emotional recrim-
inations, except for once--when he killed a
wounded buddy in Vietnam. The man was dying from
gangrene, and, as the prisoner puts it, "I owed
him. He saved my life once."
Darabont discussed the interpolated scene as

> not really a case of my trying to "im-
> prove" on King as much as it was an at-
> tempt to bring the internalized subtle-
> ties of his wonderful story out into the
> open. I really felt I needed a forum
> for presenting the main character´s
> thoughts and conflict in simple cinemat-
> ic terms. King, of course, can simply
> tell us what the guy´s thinking and
> feeling by stating it outright. Since
> one loses that ability with the camera,
> one must find other ways.
>   Thematically . . . I tried to have
> John, an inherently gentle man, sit down
> and have a good heart-to-heart with the
> darker side of his own nature, a side
> that most people barely ever glimpse,
> much less have to confront face to face.
> This darker side, of course, was em-
> bodied in the character of the prisoner.
> It was a summit meeting, so to speak,
> between a man´s finer instincts and his
> baser ones, in which compromises had to
> be reached. With this, I had hoped to
> somewhat parallel the inner dialogue
> with which King so richly endowed his
> written character.
>   Anyway, in trying to "bring the
> story out," I´m afraid I found myself

guilty of exactly the same thing that I've condemned others vehemently for doing . . . that is, modifying King's work in an extreme way to adapt it to the screen. (Letter)

In spite of the interpolated material, however, and in opposition to Darabont's self-condemnatory tone in the final paragraph of his letter, the scene works, effectively visualizing King's character's internal conflict.

This conversation is the turning point for Johnny. He makes his decision--but before he returns to the hospital room, Darabont injects a superfluous dream sequence. Johnny is reading a law book, sitting on a chair in the middle of the hospital corridor. Further down, a wheelchair rolls into the hall. He looks up. This time, a shrouded figure sits in the chair. He runs from it, but finds himself in a dead-end. The door to the stairwell is locked, so he punches the elevator button and almost falls inside when the door slides open.

At the back of the elevator he sees the chair . . . and the shrouded figure.

He pulls back the sheet and sees his mother's face, her eyes closed. He leans down and cradles the body in his arms. As he does so, the face turns to the side--and becomes a leering death's-head skull!

There is little justification for the scene, since the story is so potent without the easy fright of a sudden cut to disintegrating flesh (the same problem that afflicted the film of Straub's Ghost Story). Darabont's explanation suggests that he was aware of the underlying problems the image created:

As for the dream scene, all I can do is put on my best "aw shucks" grin and stare at my shoes. . . . If I recall correctly (I was 21 when I wrote the script, so I'm second-guessing my reasons five years after the fact), I think I wrote it in because I felt an audience might be let down by a Stephen King film without a typical Stephen King "moment." Perhaps I am guilty of underestimating

my own (and King's) audience, but the
story is pretty uncharacteristic of his
work; it certainly isn't the sort of
story people think of when they think of
Stephen King. (Letter).

Other than in that single instance, however,
Darabont's screenplay works unusually well, cap-
turing the tone of King's story. Michael Cornelison plays Johnny almost perfectly: he is strong,
yet vulnerable; he knows what he has to do, yet
cannot bring himself to do it. The closeups of
his face and eyes are particularly effective,
letting us see into his pain.

Dee Croxton as the mother also gives a fine
performance. She handles the highly pitched emo-
tionalism of the final scene well, underplaying a
bit, letting just the right stress enter her voice
when she asks for the capsule . . . "please." The
sequence with the purse works nicely, especially
since it does not seem as premeditated as in the
story--Johnny isn't as concerned with avoiding
blame for her death. When Croxton's arthritic
fingers close on the medicine container and clamp
down to insure that her prints--and only hers--are
on it, the film reaches its well-constructed climax.

The cinematography by Juan Ruiz Anchia (simple browns and yellows mostly, except for the
harsh lighting of the prison scene) and the background music (again simple, a flute playing plain-
tive not-quite-melodies) both enhance the film.

It is good news that the legal problems with
the films have been resolved. I wouldn't miss not
seeing The Boogeyman again--but The Woman in the
Room is one of the best screen adaptations of any
of King's works, a particular pleasure since the
story itself is among King's strongest. The new
Granite videocassette is worth its price; and the
sound and visual qualities are much better than on
the earlier casette.

3. "Gramma"

In March, 1985, production began on the new
hour-long Twilight Zone anthology for CBS, with
Harlan Ellison as creative consultant and a long
list of proposed episodes, including Arthur C.

152

Clarke's "The Star," Ray Bradbury's "The Burning Man," Robert Heinlein's "By His Bootstraps," Ellison's "Shatterday," and King's "Gramma."

Much as did "The Woman in the Room," "Gramma" has limited sets; an even more limited cast, appropriate for the Twilight Zone's 20-minute format; and all the atmosphere one could want. As a story, "Gramma" suffered from excess length and too much in-depth characterization because of the main character's constant reminiscences.

But on television, and especially in the Twilight Zone tradition . . . .

Even before the teleplay was filmed, publicity for the story was intense. Ellison announced that the segment would be "the most terrifying thing you will ever see on television." As evidence of the script's power, Ellison stated that the text was so frightening that secretaries were afraid to type it: "They couldn't go any further on the first reading" (Herndon, "Real Tube" 10B).

Appearing as they did in Twilight Zone Magazine, Ellison's comments might be taken· with a grain of salt; still, they contain some truth. King's story blends suspense and horror; a teleplay derived from it should represent a highlight of horror. King is cited in the same article and elsewhere as pleased with the teleplay.

As Ellison argues in his columns for The Magazine of Fantasy and Science Fiction, however, it is extremely difficult to transfer King's words into visual images. Unfortunately, "Gramma" does not prove an exception to the rules.

At first the segment looks promising, with Barrett Oliver well cast as Georgie. The mother is appropriately removed from the center of focus, both visually and symbolically. The setting works quite effectively: dusky walls, a long corridor leading to a splash of light, the boy isolated in an old-fashioned kitchen that is oddly proportioned and hence unsettling.

Almost immediately, Ellison introduces his resolution to one of the main difficulties in the text. King's story has, as Ellison notes, "no characters, no dialogue, and no action. It's all internal" (Herndon, "Real Tube" 10A). The immediate problem is how to dramatize what in King's text remains primarily internal development. Since only Georgie is present (with the exception

153

of the monstrous Gramma, of course), how can one provide essential narrative information?

Ellison answers by using voice-over. At times, the technique works well. As Georgie walks down the hall toward Gramma's room, the rational part of his mind says one thing--"I'm not going in there"--even as the irrational part impels him forward. King's tension between alternatives is reproduced nicely, with a concomittant tension between visual and verbal representation.

At other times, however, the voice-over becomes distracting as Georgie attempts to tell too much too quickly. There are, to be sure, moments without dialogue or monologue, effectively backed up with mood music. Still, the imbalance of rushing internal monologue, intercut with remembered dialogue between Georgie's uncle and his mother, deflects the viewer's attention at critical moments.

Even more threatening to the tone of the story, however, is Ellison's insistence that "Gramma" owe more to H. P. Lovecraft than to Stephen King. In the text, only the name "Hastur" connects King with Lovecraft; in Ellison's teleplay, Georgie discovers a copy of the <u>Necronomicon</u> itself--a disappointingly thin and modern-looking book--and is introduced to Cthulhu, Yog-Sothoth, and other great old ones. Georgie's finding a copy of the forbidden book beneath the floorboards of Gramma's room strains the credibility of anyone familiar with the history of that accursed volume. At the same time, Georgie reads Gramma's journal too quickly for credibility and understands too easily that she is a "witch"--not exactly the best term to use for a narrative set within the Lovecraft mythos.

Other elements disturb as well. The text gives no explanation as to how or why Gramma sucks Georgie's shadow into her room; the episode seems primarily a foreshadowing of Georgie's final "consumption." While the sets are highly evocative of horror, other points seem more conventional. When Georgie opens the floorboards to the accompaniment of a rather trite burst of light, he unnecessarily exclaims (and explains), "That could have got me. It could have burnt my head off. But nothing's on fire." His actions fully communicate his point. There was no need for the voice-over at all.

Similarly, when the apparently dead Gramma grabs Georgie´s wrist, the moment suffers from being too expected--a problem present in King´s story, as a matter of fact. Nothing else could happen, given the camera angle and the way Georgie´s arm must cross Gramma´s. When Gramma pulls him toward her, the film wisely does not try to define her beyond suggestions of monstrous forms; when Georgie is pulled into her, however, the spinning picture does not represent effectively what happens.

The weakest scene occurs when the mother returns. As soon as we see Georgie at the table, head down, face averted, we know that there is a problem. The mother suddenly becomes the center of action, with Georgie either peripheral or out of the scene entirely. In a scene designed to heighten the terror, the boy turns toward the camera. As the mother says that "Gramma will always be with us," he opens his eyes to reveal the alien eyes we have already associated with Gramma. Unfortunately, the scene is too stock for the effect it hopes to create. Even as he turns his head, we already know what we will see.

The episode more closely resembles Lovecraft than King. It is both confirmatory and revelatory, an example of the "terminal climax" common in Lovecraft´s works, in which the final line both concludes the story and reveals the horror. The technique is rarer in King; in fact, his more leisurely and subtle conclusion to "Gramma" instills greater fear in the reader, as Georgie simply lies back and thinks to himself what he can now do to his older brother.

The segment received a number of highly positive reviews. Kent Daniel Bentkowski argued, for example, that "both Ellison and director Bradford May made certain that anyone who tuned in would fall witness to the highest order of state of the art terror, and [thus] be greatly affected by this most disturbing foray into the dimension of death and insanity" ("King´s ´Gramma´" 5).

My reactions were more reserved. Staging, casting, and special effects contributed to a generally effective production. Occasional humor broke the increasing tension: Georgie´s promise that if God gets him out of this he´ll never use

155

the F-word again, or his comment that the old books are probably written in French or some other old language. But the rush of trying to fit the story into 20 minutes worked against it. The voice-overs were at times difficult to understand. And the Lovecraftian elements--especially Georgie discovering the Necronomicon--seemed bothersome.

Ellison's teleplay nevertheless succeeded in adapting a difficult story for television. The segment contains sufficient dramatic tension, as well as authentically startling moments, to keep viewers watching and attentive.

NOTES

[1]An earlier discussion of "The Boogeyman" and "The Woman in the Room" appeared as a letter in Castle Rock (September 1985).

CHAPTER XV

Films in Production:
Overdrive, Pet Sematary, The Stand, and Others

As should have become immediately apparent to
anyone reaching this point in The Films of Stephen
King, interest in King's fictions as film properties has grown almost as intense as the interest
in his novels. The beginning was slow: Carrie in
1976, then a three-year hiatus before Salem's Lot
in 1979. The Shining appeared in 1980; then
again, a lapse of some time before Creepshow in
1982. The Boogeyman was also completed that year.
In 1983, the momentum of King's own writing
spilled over into films; in what could legitimate-
ly be considered an annus mirabilis, King completed first drafts of three novels and a screenplay; published two novels (Christine and Pet
Sematary) and a novella (Cycle of the Werewolf),
as well as several short stories; Frank Darabont
completed The Woman in the Room; and three feature-length, major-budget films appeared: Teague's
Cujo, Cronenberg's Dead Zone, and Carpenter's
Christine.
In 1984, the momentum continued with Children
of the Corn, and Firestarter. As flawed as either
may be, both nevertheless indicate the unflagging,
if not increasing, awareness that King could be
big business at the theater as well as at the
bookstore. The original videocassette release of
The Boogeyman and The Woman in the Room took place
during 1984; the cassette was, however, subsequently withdrawn. The year was capped off by the
late November release date for "The Word Processor of the Gods" on Tales from the Darkside,
King's first appearance in a television anthology
format.
By 1985, King's importance to filmmaking had
been clearly established--and then the rules
changed. Cat's Eye appeared, the first feature
film since Creepshow to be based on King's screenplay. Later the same year, Silver Bullet was released as the film which King called his first

"´movie´ movie"--that is, a full-length film that
breaks from the anthology format of <u>Creepshow</u> and
<u>Cat´s Eye</u> by developing a single, unified narra-
tive.

Although no year has quite matched 1983 for
sheer output, development of King´s fictions as
films has not particularly slowed. The first
months of 1986 saw the broadcast of Ellison´s
"Gramma" and the official release of <u>The Woman in
the Room</u> and <u>The Boogeyman</u>. Even more critically,
in July, two major films will be released: King´s
directorial debut in <u>Overdrive</u> and Rob Reiner´s
prouction of <u>The Body</u>. And additional films are
in various stages of production as well, with
varying degrees of involvement from King. Some
are based on King treatments, others on fully developed screenplays; in a few instances, he will
have a much more extensive hand in the final productions, although he has declared in several
interviews that he is not interested in directing
a second film quite yet. Perhaps later, he
explains, but not now: "I can imagine doing it
again. But I can´t imagine doing it again very
soon" (Hewitt "Overdrive" 9).

Simply in terms of numbers, films made from
King´s works have become important, both as films
and as cultural indicators. Most have performed
respectably at the box office, although King has
noted that the trend has been a downward spiral,
from the strong financial showing of Kubrick´s <u>The
Stand</u> to <u>Cat´s Eye</u>´s disappointingly weak returns.

With the number--and kinds--of films now in
production, that tendency may be reversed, since
several of the films soon to appear are based on
the most intriguing and powerful of King´s fictions.

1. Overdrive

In the beginning, <u>Overdrive</u> was "Trucks," a
short story from the <u>Night Shift</u> collection that
King considered among his favorite stories. Then
it was a screenplay, also called "Trucks," then
re-titled <u>Maximum Overdrive</u>. Dino De Laurentiis
optioned rights to the screenplay, and eventually,
King agreed to direct the film, finally (apparently) to be called <u>Overdrive</u>.

Since the production of <u>Creepshow</u>, King had

occasionally mentioned his desire to direct. In an interview with R. H. Martin, King said that he had spent a good deal of time on the Creepshow set, not so much to see that "no one mutilated my baby," but in order to learn directorial techniques by observing and working with George A. Romero. Four years later, his opportunity to use that training came when Overdrive went into production ("Stephen King" 11).

With King working as both screenwriter and director, Overdrive has become an intriguing project. For the first time, King will have a substantial effect on the final product, although De Laurentiis retains control over the final cut (Hewitt, "Overdrive" 9). This is, of course, a double-edged sword. Overdrive will clearly reflect King's individual vision in ways that Creepshow, Cat's Eye, and Silver Bullet could not; what will emerge should be a clearer definition of Stephen King as filmmaker.

On the other hand, however, his dual role (triple-role, if one counts his having written the original property on which the screenplay is based) gives Overdrive a notoriety that may work against it. King realizes that his name on the film as director provides a "built-in draw; the idea that people will come to see the film the way they come to see the two-headed cow" (Martin, "Stephen King" 11). More seriously, Overdrive will represent Stephen King brought to the screen exactly the way Stephen King would wish it. If the film does not succeed, there will be no one to lay blame on--no idiosyncratic directors, eccentric screenplays, etc.

It is dangerous, of course, to generalize about a film in production on the basis of a first-draft screenplay. The publication of Silver Bullet by Signet in late 1985 graphically illustrates the changes that can infiltrate a narrative between conception and production, even when the author is closely involved with filming.

Even so, Overdrive is a promising film. In the original script, dated February 1985, and still titled "Trucks," King has merged several of his stories, then amplified them with original material. The core story, "Trucks," remains virtually intact, but the scope has enlarged immensely. It is no longer simply a tale about trucks assert-

ing independence and quasi-sentience; it has become, in King's own terms, a "mechanical Birds,
heavily influenced by Hitchcock's films about
birds suddenly gone murderous.

With King, however, the threat isn't birds or
even just trucks, as in the short story. All machines suddenly come to life and attack their human creators. King isn't particularly concerned
in defining a rationale for the attacks. In what
may be the weakest element in the screenplay,
Overdrive blames the unexpected destructive streak
on a passing comet, a film cliche central to
earlier films such as The Day of the Triffids and
exploited occasionally since. As if recognizing
the inherent triteness of the situation, King
simply asserts the comet's presence in the opening
lines of the script, noting that Earth will remain
in the tail of the comet for a little over eight
days. That, we may assume, will bracket the time
of the comet's effects on the berserk machinery.
The whole situation does, however, seem weak, in
spite of King's contention that providing a rationale for the horror to come is not critical: "I
said, what would cause that [the machines to go
crazy]? And I tossed that out 'cause you can
always think of something" (Hewitt "Overdrive").
Unfortunately, he may be a bit too cavalier about
causation; it is the kind of technical point that
viewers (and critics) frequently fasten upon.

In spite of the causation, however, the fact
remains that in Overdrive machinery of all sorts
runs amok. Beyond merely the gas-hungry trucks
that blockade the Dixie Boy diner, viewers will be
treated to a host of other murderous devices as
well: "A man is clipped to death by his own power
mower. A neighbor has his mind blown by a mal-
functioning Walkman, and a waitress is carved up
by a knife" (Garcia). Mechanical monsters gone
crazy provide most of the action in Overdrive, and
King notes that having an R-rating for the film
gives him great leeway in creating appropriately
horrific effects:

> heads will roll, bodies will get mashed
> under trucks, people will get cut up by
> electric knives that turn themselves on;
> hopefully, there'll be an older gentle-
> man who is battered to death by bat-

160

tery-driven toy cars. (Martin, "Overdrive" 12)

In the opening moments of the script, for example, a digital time-temperature clock on a local
bank flashes obscene messages to passersby; an
auto-teller calls a customer an unpleasant name
via its computer screen; and a drawbridge takes it
upon itself to raise without giving drivers
warning--the result is a concatenation of death,
destruction, and crushed vehicles when brakes give
way as the bridge roadway angles up more and more
steeply. Although it could conceivably be cut
from the final script--largely because of the
expense involved--the scene sets the tone for
Overdrive.

Other motifs in the script are reminiscent of
earlier King treatments: the death-dealing toy
soldiers in "Battleground"; the ambulatory laun-
dry-monster in "The Mangler"; Harold Parkette's
threatening silver Lawnboy mower in "The Lawnmower
Man"--all stories which, with "Trucks," were col-
lected in Night Shift. And, of course, if Christine herself is not among the antagonists, her
cousins certainly are.

In addition, an episode in the screenplay may
suggest one of King's next novels. The Tommyknockers, scheduled for publication in 1987, replaces organic monsters with mechanical gadgets.
"The Revelations of 'Becka Paulson," an excerpt
published in Rolling Stone and reprinted in the
Scream Press limited edition of Skeleton Crew,
gives a taste of what the novel will be like.
Elsewhere, King has commented that any "monsters"
in The Tommyknockers have been dead millions of
years; what confronts his characters are monsters
we have created for ourselves.

In an interview with Charles Grant in 1985,
King apparently refers to The Tommyknockers when
he mentions a passage in a novel he has been writing "off and on for a long, long time." A Coca-
Cola dispensing machine, suddenly come to life and
equipped with computer memory chips, "levitates
and cruises around the country roads, very slowly
in this ghastly silence--this red and white Coke
machine with the sun glimmering off the glass
panel from which the bottles come out. Every now
and then it will find a pedestrian and run him

down" ("King-Size Interview" 28).

In the original script treatment for <u>Over-drive</u>, one dramatic encounter includes a berserk soft drink vending machine, much like the one in King´s manuscript. Instead of cruising along and smashing into characters, however, this one fires cans from the dispensing slot--so fast that they become lethal projectiles, smashing into heads and backs and generally wreaking havoc. Ironically (or perhaps not so much so), the dispenser is on the set of a movie stage in Dino De Laurentiis´s studios; by the end of the scene, the entire studio has been destroyed, climaxing with a huge truck smashing its way into De Laurentiis´s own office.

These details suggest that the film has grown beyond the rather sketchy narrative of "Trucks." There is now a rationale for the situation, an exploration of how extensive the effects have been, and the possibility of a happy ending, unlike the pessimistically indeterminate closing of the short story.

The script reads well and promises a healthy helping of suspense and action, along with the heads rolling, bodies smashed, etc., . . . and will be brought to life by a strong cast. Pat Hingle and Laura Harrington fill primary roles, with Emilio Estevez starring as Bill Robertson, the short-order cook at the Dixie Boy diner and star of the film. Estevez has built a following of his own through such films as <u>The Repo Man</u>. As Martin Sheen´s son, however, he also continues a tradition of association with King films; his brooding presence may be as impressive and as critical as the older Sheen´s in <u>Dead Zone</u>.

The production crew also includes familiar names. De Laurentiis is involved with his fifth Stephen King property, following <u>Dead Zone</u>, <u>Fire-starter</u>, <u>Cat´s Eye</u>, and <u>Silver Bullet</u>. Martha Schumacher (<u>Silver Bullet</u>) will again be producer, with Armando Nannuzzi as cinematographer and award-winning stuntman Julius LeFlore in charge of stuntwork.

<u>Overdrive</u> is well into production; the release date has been set for July 18, 1986. From all indications, it promises to be an effective film, coupling King´s storytelling power with visual images that emphasize the film´s theme: man

162

versus machine. And, as happens so frequently in King´s fiction, it is not always certain which will emerge victorious.

2. Pet Sematary

King did not like Pet Sematary from the beginning. The novel was, he thought, "too gross to ever be published." The relationship between Louis and Gage Creed was painful, "from the time the book was written, through the rewriting, and right through the publishing process" (Martin, "Overdrive" 12). His few comments about the book at the 1984 International Conference on the Fantastic in the Arts, along with Douglas Winter´s accompanying discussion of how Pet Sematary came to be published, made it clear that King was not willing to discuss the novel. Elsewhere, King simply referred to the novel as obscene because of its unalleviated darkness and despair.

Why, then, is it now beginning production as a film, with King heavily involved in the project as screenwriter.

"It occurred to me one night," King says,

> that it would make a wonderful picture for George Romero, that it could be a synthesis of his Dead pictures and Martin, which I think is his finest picture to date. And, in between those two things, there was also a place to produce a picture with the kind of grossness that The Exorcist has. And, if we did it through Laurel, I felt that it could be done almost on a cottage industry basis, allowing me to participate not just in writing, but in the production, including the casting and all that other stuff, so I decided to go ahead. (Martin, "Overdrive" 12).

The property does seem ideal for Romero, and certainly represents King at his darkest and most oppressive. Much of the novel was autobiographical (cf. Collings, MFSK 85-93), and consequently more intense for King to work with than externalized, distanced topics, such as vampires or ghosts or haunted cars. In writing the screenplay, however, he noted that much of that subjectivity had passed. His children were older, his "Gage" no longer a child threatened by trucks passing their home. As a result, the script was less difficult to work with than one might expect.

In the first-draft version of the screenplay, these points come through clearly. The script follows the novel closely, streamlined, of course, to accommodate the narrative into film format. Norma Crandall disappears, for example; Jud mentions that she died some time before the Creeds moved in. Her disappearance from the narrative decreases the poignancy the novel explores so carefully; to that extent, the film seems less a meditation on death and change than the novel.

On the other hand, King compensates for her loss by incorporating Victor Pascow´s ghost more fully into the script as a counter-balance to the evil of the Pet Sematary. He appears to others besides Louis and provides a clearly defined alternative to the horror entailed in Louis´s refusal to accept death.

The critical scenes--Gage´s death, Jud Crandall´s death, Rachel´s death--are exceptionally well handled in the screenplay. King lightens the visual impact of horror; we do not actually see Gage struck by the truck, for example, but rather understand what has happened through intercut still photographs of Gage as a child and of the moments just before his death. Rachel´s death takes place in darkness; when Louis discovers her body, he sees only a single limb dangling from an attic entryway.

In addition, the opening shots articulate more completely and literally the "presence" in the Pet Sematary. Light and dark, patterns of shadow, back- and under-lighting suggest a face in the deadfall just beyond the cemetery, so that from the beginning of the film, viewers are more aware of what powers Louis Creed must oppose.

Otherwise, the first-draft script remains true to the original. There have been no major alterations, and King has retained what may be the most horrific line in contemporary dark fantasy: Rachel´s final word to Louis Creed.

Production of Pet Sematary has been delayed for a number of reasons. Nor have any decisions on casting been announced. Romero has indicated

that at least parts of the film will be shot in
Maine, with work possibly beginning in spring of
1986.

Given the powerful narrative and the incremental, irrevocable horror of the novel itself,
Pet Sematary promises to be perhaps the first film
from a King property to retain entirely the sense
of the original. If treated with a casual emphasis on visual blood and gore, with occasional moments of fright thrown in, it could be eminently
disappointing. If handled carefully, however--and
there is every indication that King and Romero in-
tend to do so--it could be a film that is at once
intense and truly horrifying.

3. The Stand

The Stand was the first property King and
Romero considered working on. King agreed to provide a working screenplay; the result was over 400
pages long, enough for a film running in excess of
six hours. At one point, they considered doing
two films, one based on the flu epidemic, the second following events in Boulder and Las Vegas.
King believed that

> it would be possible to build a big ar-
> tificial climax in the middle that would
> satisfy audiences for the time being.
> If it was all shot at once, the films
> could be released maybe 3 months or a
> season apart. (Grant "King-Size Inter-
> view" 29)

The final decision, however, was to try for a
single feature-length film. King is now working
on a fourth revision of the script, consolidating
a number of characters from the book into single
characters in the script, streamlining the narrative and, in consequence, transforming it into
something new. Unlike The Dead Zone or Christine,
The Stand has neither a single character nor a
severely limited number of characters as the
focus. It is a large, sprawling work, intimately
concerned with dozens of individuals. To transfer
it to screen will require more a translation than
an adaptation. It will, no doubt, be fascinating
and exciting, but it will not be The Stand that

readers may expect.

4. Other Films in Production

Rob Reiner has completed most of the work on _The Body_, with its release scheduled for July 18, 1986. Other than notes in _Castle Rock_, however, little information is available, except that a recent preview was well received.

The May issue of _Castle Rock_ also announced that _IT_ will be televised as a mini-series on ABC-TV in fall of 1987. Although a mini-series is probably the best way to do justice to the complexity of _IT_, the constraints of television standards, as well as the need for commercial interruptions, may weaken King's narrative greatly, as occurred with Kobritz's _Salem's Lot_. It is exciting, however, that one of King's most important novels will be presented as a film as well.

Recent issues of _Fangoria_ have also mentioned another project. King's _Training Exercise_ is scheduled for production by De Laurentiis's North Carolina studios. The plot involves a young man who flies to a Pacific island for "training exercises" conducted by veterans of World War II and the Korean War--only to discover that the exercises are for real. The film will probably appear in 1987.

Production information on Taft Entertainment's production of _The Running Man_ is also sketchy. The Bachman novel was originally to be filmed in Canada, with Christopher Reeve in the starring role. The most recent information, however, is that filming has been shifted to Los Angeles and that Arnold Schwarzenegger is being considered for the lead.

Finally, _The Talisman_ has been discussed as a possible Steven Spielberg property; beyond that, no definite information is available.

This listing is not intended as a complete survey, of course. Other King novels and stories are no doubt being considered, discussed, and negotiated. Still, it does indicate the continuing interest in bringing King's words to film.

166

FILMOGRAPHY

The Boogeyman

Tantalus, 1982, 1984.   VHS: $79.95.   30 minutes.

Jeffrey C. Schiro, producer.
Jeffrey C. Schiro, director.
Jeffrey C. Schiro, screenwriter.
Jeffrey C. Schiro, editor.
Douglas Meltzer, director of photography.
John Cote, music.
Jeff Schiro and John Cote, sound design.
Susan Schiro, set design.

Cast: Michael Reid. . . . . .Lester Billings
      Bert Linder . . . . .Dr. Harper
      Terence Brady . . . . Sgt. Copeland
      Mindy Silverman . . . . Rita Billings
      Jerome Bynder . . . . Coroner
      Bobby Perschell . . . . Denny
      Michael Dragosin. . . . . .Andy
      Nancy Lindberg. . . . . Neighbor
      James Holmes. . . . . Husband
      John Macdonald. . . . . .Cop #1
      Dave Burr . . . . .Cop #2
      Rich West . . . . .Attendant #1
      John Cote . . . . .Attendant #2
      Brooke Trivas . . . . .Dispatch nurse

Produced in association with the New York University School of Undergraduate Film.   Produced on
videocassette as "Two Mini-Features from . . . .
Stephen King´s Night Shift Collection" (includes
The Woman in the Room).

Carrie.

United Artists, 1976; CBS/Fox Video. Beta, VHS
$69.95; Laser $29.98; CED $19.98. 97 minutes.
Rating: R.

Paul Monash, producer.
Louis A. Stroller, associate producer.
Brian De Palma, director.
Lawrence D. Cohen, screenwriter.
Pino Donaggio, music.
Mario Tosi, photography.
William Kenny and Jack Fisk, art directors.
Paul Hirsch, editor.

Cast: Sissy Spacek . . . . Carrie White
      Piper Laurie . . . . Margaret White
      Amy Irving . . . . .Sue Snell
      William Katz . . . . Tommy Ross
      Nancy Allen . . . . . . .Chris Hargensen
      John Travoltra . . . . . . .Billy Nolan
      Betty Buckley . . . . Miss Collins
      P.J. Soles . . . . .Norma
      Priscilla Pointer. . . . . . .Mrs. Snell
      Stephen Gienash. . . . . . . Mr. Morton

Cat´s Eye.

MGM/United Artists, 1984.   Beta, VHS: $79.95.   94
minutes. Rating: PG-13.

Martha Schumacher, producer.
Milton Subotsky, co-producer.
Dino de Laurentiis, executive producer.
John M. Eckert, production executive.
Lewis Teague, director.
Stephen King, screenwriter.
Jack Cardiff, director of photography.
Giorgio Postiglione, production design.
Alan Silvestri, music.
Scott Conrad, film editor.
Carlo Rambaldi, creator of creatures.
Jeff Jarvis, special effects coordinator.
Barry Nolan, special visual effects.

Cast: Drew Barrymore. . . . . Amanda
      James Woods . . . . .Morrison
      Alan King . . . . .Dr. Donati
      Kenneth McMillan. . . . . .Cressner
      Robert Hays . . . . .Norris
      Candy Clark . . . . Sally Ann
      James Naughton. . . . . .Hugh
      Tony Munafo . . . . .Junk
      Court Miller. . . . . .Mr. McCann
      Russell Horton. . . . . Mr. Milquetoast
      Patricia Benson . . . . . . .Mrs. Milquetoast
      Mary D´Arcy . . . . Cindy
      James Rebhorn . . . . . . Drunken businessman
      Jack Dillon . . . . Janitor
      Susan Hawes . . . . Mrs. McCann
      Shelley Burch . . . . .Jerrilyn
      Sal Richards. . . . . .Westlake
      Jesse Doran . . . . .Albert
      Patricia Kalember . . . . .Marcia
      Mike Starr. . . . . Ducky
      Charles Dutton. . . . . Don

Filmed on location in Wilmington, NC.

"Quitter´s Inc.": 38 minutes
"The Ledge": 26 minutes
"The General": 30 minutes

Children of the Corn

New World Pictures, 1984. In association with Angeles Entertainment Group; Inverness Productions,
Inc.; Hal Roach Studios; Cinema Group Ventures. A
Gatlin Production. VHS, Beta: $69.95; Laser:
$34.95; CED: $19.95. 93 minutes. Rating: R.

Donald P. Borchers and Terrence Kirby, producers.
Mark Lipson, associate producer.
Earl Glick and Charles K. Weber, executive pro-
    ducers.
Fritz Kiersch, director.
George Goldsmith, screenwriter.
Patience Thoreson and Frankie Nixon, script sup-
    plements.
Raoul Lomas, director of photography.
Jonathan Elias, music.
Harry Keramidas, film editor.
Craig Stearns, art director.
Max W. Anderson, special visual effects.
SPFX, Inc. and Eric Rumsey, special effects.

Cast: Peter Horton. . . . . Burt
    Linda Hamilton. . . . . Vicky
    R. G. Anthony . . . . .Diesel
    John Franklin. . . . . .Isaac
    Courtenay Gains. . . . . Malachi
    Robby Kiger. . . . . .Job
    Annemarie McEvoy . . . . .Sarah
    Julie Maddalena. . . . . Rachel
    Jonas Marlowe. . . . . Joseph
    John Philbin . . . . Amos
    Dan Snook. . . . . .Boy
    David Cowen. . . . . .Dad
    Suzy Southam . . . . .Mom
    D. G. Johnson. . . . . Mr. Hansen
    Patrick Boylan . . . . . . .Hansen´s customer
    Elmer Soderstrom . . . . . .Hansen´s customer
    Teresa Coigo . . . . .Hansen´s customer
    Mitch Carter . . . . .Radio Preacher

Filmed on locations in Sioux City, Whiting, Salix,
and Hernick Iowa. Budget: $3,000,000.

Christine.

Columbia Pictures, 1983. Beta, VHS: $79.95; Laser: $29.95; CED: $29.95. 110 minutes. Rating: R.

Richard Kobritz, producer.
Larry Franco, co-producer.
Barry Bernardi, associate producer.
Kirby McCauley and Mark Tarlov, executive producers.
John Carpenter, director.
Bill Phillips, screenwriter.
Donald M. Morgan, director of photography.
Daniel Lomino, production design.
John Carpenter, in association with Alan Howarth, music.
Marion Rothman, editor.
Roy Arbogast, special effects.
William Joseph Durrell, Jr., set design.

Cast: Keith Gordon . . . . Arnie Cunningham
      John Stockwell. . . . . .Dennis Guilder
      Alexandra Paul. . . . . Leigh Cabot
      Robert Prosky . . . . .Will Darnell
      Harry Dean Stanton. . . . . Rudolph Junkins
      Christine Belford . . . . . Regina Cunningham
      Roberts Blossom . . . . George Le Bay
      William Ostrander . . . . . Buddy Repperton
      David Spielberg . . . . Mr. Casey
      Malcolm Danare. . . . . . . .Moochie Morgan
      Steven Tash . . . . .Rich
      Stuart Charns . . . . .Vandenberg
      Kelly Preston . . . . .Roseanne
      Marc Poppel . . . . Chuck
      Robert Darnell. . . . . .Michael Cunningham
      Douglas Warhit. . . . . Bemis
      Bruce French . . . . .Mr. Smith
      Keri Montgomery. . . . . .Effie

Shot on location in Los Angeles and Anaheim, CA; Oak Park High School, Agoura CA.

Budget: $10,000,000 ($500,000 for special effects).

Creepshow.

Warner Brothers, 1982: United Film Distribution;
Laurel Productions. Warner Home Video: VHS
$69.95; Beta; CED $29.95. 120 minutes. Rating:
R.

Richard P. Rubenstein, producer.
David E. Vogel, associate producer.
Salah M. Hassanein, executive producer.
George A. Romero, director.
Stephen King, screenwriter.
Michael Gornick, director of photography.
Cletus Anderson, production design and special
    effects.
John Harrison, music.
Pasquale Buba, Paul Hirsch, George A. Romero,
    Michael Spolan: editors
Tom Savini, make-up.
Jack Kamen, comic book art.

Cast: Prologue/Epilogue:

      Iva Jean Saracen . . . . Billy´s mother
      Joe King . . . . .Billy

      "Father´s Day" (17 minutes): Michael Spolan,
      editor.

      Carrie Nye . . . . .Sylvia Grantham
      Viveca Lindfors. . . . . Aunt Bedelia
      Ed Harris . . . . .Hank Blaine
      Warner Shook . . . . Richard Grantham
      Elizabeth Regan. . . . . .Cass Blaine
      Jan Lormer . . . . .Nathan Grantham
      John Amplas. . . . . .Nathan´s Corpse
      Nan Magg . . . . Mrs. Danvers
      Peter Messer . . . . Yarbro

      "The Lonesome Death of Jordy Verrill" (14
      minutes): Pasquale Buba, editor.

      Stephen King . . . . .Jordy Verrill
      Bingo O´Malley . . . . Jordy´s father
                          Professor
                            Doctor

George A. Romero, editor.

Leslie Nielson . . . . .Richard Vickers
Ted Danson . . . . .Harry Wentworth
Gaylen Ross. . . . . .Becky Vickers

"The Crate" (37 minutes): Paul Hirsch, editor.

Hal Holbrook . . . . Harry Northrup
Adrienne Barbeau . . . . Wilma Northrup
Fritz Weaver . . . . Dexter Stanley
Robert Harper. . . . . .Charlie Gereson
Don Keefer . . . . Mike the Janitor
Christine Forrest. . . . . . .Tabitha Raymond
Chuck Aber . . . . .Richard Raymond
Cletus Anderson. . . . . Host
Katie Kalowitz . . . . Maid

"They're Creeping Up on You" (14 minutes): Michael Spolan, editor.

E.G. Marshall . . . . Upson Pratt
David Early . . . . White

Epilogue
Garbage Man #1. . . . . .Marti Schiff
Garbage Man #2. . . . . .Tom Savini

Budget: $8,000,000.

Cujo.

Warner Communications; Taft Entertainment, 1983.
Beta, VHS: $69.95; CED: $29.95. 120 minutes.
Rating: R.

Daniel H. Blatt and Robert Singer, producers.
Neil A. Machlis, associate producer.
Lewis Teague, director.
Don Carlos Dunaway and Lauren Currier (Barbara
    Turner), screenwriters.
Jan de Bont, director of photography.
Guy Comtois, production designer.
Neil Travis, film editor
Charles Bernstein, music.
Peter Knowlton, visual effects makeup.
Karl Lewis Miller, animal action director.
Judith Holstra and Marcia S. Ross, casting.

Cast: Dee Wallace . . . . .Donna Trenton
    Daniel Hugh-Kelly. . . . . . . Victor Trenton
    Christopher Stone. . . . . Steve Kemp
    Ed Lauter. . . . . Joe Camber
    Kaiulani Lee . . . . Charity Camber
    Mills Watson . . . . Gary Pervier
    Danny Pintauro . . . . .Tad Trenton
    Billy Jacoby . . . . Brett Camber
    Sandy Ward . . . . .Sheriff Bannerman
    Jerry Mardin . . . . .Masen
    Merritt Olsen. . . . .Sharps Cereal Professor
    Arthur Rosenberg . . . . . . Roger Breakstone
    Terry Donovan-Smith. . . . . .Marry
    Robert Elross. . . . . .Meara
    Robert Behling . . . . Fournier
    Claire Nons. . . . . Lady Professor
    David H. Blatt . . . . .Dr. Merkolt

The film was shot on location in Petaluma and San-
ta Rosa, Mendocino County, California.

Budget: $5,000,000 (earned over $6,000,000 in
first three days of release).

Dead Zone.

Paramount Pictures, 1983. Beta, VHS ($59.95);
Laser ($29.95); CED ($29.95). 103 minutes. Rating:
R.

Debra Hill, producer.
Jeffrey Chernov, associate producer.
Dino de Laurentiis, executive producer.
David Cronenberg, director.
Jeffrey Boam, screenwriter.
Mark Irwin, director of photography.
Carol Spier, production design.
Michael Kamen, music.
Ronald Sanders, film editor.
John Belyeu, special effects coordinator.

Cast: Christopher Walken . . . . . Johnny Smith
      Brooke Adams . . . . Sarah Bracknell
      Tom Skerrit. . . . . Bannerman
      Herbert Lom. . . . . . . .Dr. Sam Weizak
      Anthony Zerbe. . . . . . . .Roger Stuart
      Colleen Dewhurst . . . . .Henrietta Dodd
      Nicholas Campbell. . . . . . .Frank Dodd
      Martin Sheen . . . . Greg Stillson
      Sean Sullivan. . . . . .Herb Smith
      Jackie Burroughs . . . . . . .Vera Smith
      Geza Kovacs. . . . . .Sonny Ellman
      Robert Weiss . . . . . . .Alma Frechette
      Simon Craig. . . . . .Chris Stuart
      Peter Dvorsky. . . . . .Dardis
      Julie-Ann Heathwood . . . . .Amy
      Barry Flatman. . . . . .Walt
      Raffi Tchalikian. . . . . .Denny
      Kenneth Pogue. . . . . . .Vice President
      Gordon Jocelyn . . . . . Five-star general
      Bill Copeland. . . . . .Secretary of State
      Jack Messinger . . . . Therapist
      Chapelle Jaffe. . . . . .Nurse
      Cindy Hines. . . . . Natalie
      Helene Udy . . . . Weizak´s mother
      Ramon Estevez. . .Teen-age boy with camera
      Joseph Damenchini. . . . . . .Young Weizak
      Roger Dunn . . . . .Reporter
      Wally Bondarento . . . . .Reporter
      Claude Rae . . . . .Reporter
      John Koensgen. . . . . . . .TV anchorman

```
Les Carlson. . . . . . . . . . . . Brenner
Jim Bearden . . . . . . . . . . . .Deputy
Hardee Lineham . . . . . . . . . . .Deputy
William Davis. . . . . .Ambulance driver
Sierge LeBlanc . . . . . . . . .Denny #2
Vera Winiouski . . . . . .Polish peasant
John Kopnaiko. . . . . . .Polish peasant
Dave Rigby . . . . . . . . . .Truck driver
Cathy Scorsese . . . . Model for stills of
                        Debbie Linderman
```

Shot on location at Niagara-on-the-Lake, Exbridge, Stouffville, and Toronto (January-March 1983).

Budget: $10,000,000.

Firestarter

Universal Pictures, 1984. In association with Dino de Laurentiis. Beta, VHS: $79.95; CED $29.98. 115 minutes. Rating: R.

Frank Capra, Jr., producer.
Martha Schumacher, associate producer.
Mark Lester, Director.
Stanley Mann, screenwriter.
Guiseppe Ruzzolini, director of photography.
Giorgio Postiglione, art director.
Tangerine Dream, music.
David Rawlins, editor.
Ron Sanders, co-editor.
Glenn Randall, stunt coordinator.
Mike Wood and Jeff Jarvis, special effects.
Jose Sanchez, makeup effects.
Van der Veer Photo Effects, optical effects.

Cast: David Keith . . . . Andrew McGee
Drew Barrymore. . . . . Charlie McGee
Freddie Jones . . . . . . .Dr. Joseph Wanless
Heather Locklear. . . . . Vicky McGee
Martin Sheen. . . . . Captain Hollister
George C. Scott . . . . John Rainbird
Art Carney. . . . . Irv Manders
Louise Fletcher . . . . Norma Manders
Moses Gunn. . . . . Dr. Pynchot
Antonio Vargas. . . . . Taxi Driver
Orville Jamieson. . . . . Drew Snyder
Curtis Credel . . . . Bates
Keith Colbert . . . . .Mayo
Richard Warlock . . . . Knowles
Jeff Ramsey . . . . .Steinowitz
Jack Manger . . . . .Young serviceman
Lisa Ann Barnes . . . Young serviceman's girl
Larry Sprinkle. . . . . . . .Security guard
Cassandra Ward-Freeman. . . .Woman in stall
Scott R. Davis. . . . . . . Bearded student
Nina Jones. . . . . .Grad assistant
William Alspaugh. . . . . .Proprieter
Laurens Moore . . . . Old man
Anne Fitzgibbon . . . . .Old lady
Steve Boles . . . . Mailman
Stanley Mann. . . . . Motel owner
Robert Miano. . . . . Blinded agent

```
Leon Rippy. . . . . . . . . . Blinded agent
Carole Francisco. . . . . . . . . .Joan Dugan
Wendie Womble . . . . . . . . . . . . . Josie
Etan Boritzer . . . . . . . . .DSI technician
Joan Foley. . . . . . . . . .DSI technician
John Sanderford . . . . . . . . . . .Albright
Orwin Hardy . . . . . . . . . . . DSI orderly
George Wilbur . . . . . . . . . DSI orderly
Carey Fox . . . . . . . . . . . . .Agent Hunt
```

Filmed on locations in Wilmington, NC, and the Orton Plantation.

Budget: $15,000,000.

Gramma

CBS, <u>Twilight Zone</u> series.   14 February 1986.

Philip de Guere, executive producer.
James Crocker, supervision producer (series).
Harlan Ellison, creative consultant (series).
Alan Brennert, executive story consultant.
Bradford May, director.
Harlan Ellison, teleplay.
Rockne S. O´Banon, story editor.

<u>Cast</u>: Barrett Oliver . . . . George
      Darl Anne Fluegel . . . . Mother
      Frederick Long. . . . . .Voice

Salem's Lot.

Warner Brothers, 1979 (television mini-series). Beta, VHS: $59.95.

Richard Kobritz, producer.
Anna Cottle, associate producer.
Stirling Silliphant, executive producer*
Tobe Hooper, director.
Paul Monash, teleplay.
Jules Brenner, director of photography.
Mort Rabinowitz, production design.
Harry Sukman, music.
Carroll Sax, editor.
Frank Torro, special effects.

Cast: David Soul . . . . Ben Mears
      James Mason . . . . Richard Straker
      Lance Kerwin. . . . . Mark Petrie
      Bonnie Bedelia. . . . . . . .Susan Norton
      Lew Ayres . . . . Jason Burke
      Reggie Nalder . . . . .Barlow
      Julie Cobb. . . . . Bonnie Sawyer
      Elisha Cook . . . . .Weasel Philips
      George Dzundza. . . . . . . Cullen Sawyer
      Ed Flanders . . . . Bill Norton
      Clarissa Kaye . . . . . . .Marjorie Glick
      Geoffrey Lewis. . . . . . . .Mike Ryerson
      Barney McFadden . . . . . . .Ned Tebbetts
      Kenneth McMillan. . . . . Chief Gillespie
      Fred Willard. . . . . . . .Larry Crockett
      Marie Windsor . . . . .Eva Miller
      Barbara Babcock . . . . June Petrie
      Bonnie Bartlett . . . . .Ann Norton
      Joshua Bryant . . . . .Ted Petrie
      James Gallery . . . . . . Father Callahan
      Robert Lussier. . . . . . . Nolly Gardner
      Brad Savage . . . . Danny Glick
      Ronnie Scribner . . . . . . Ralphie Glick
      Ned Wilson. . . . . Henry Glick

Location: Ferndale, CA; San Fernando Valley Mission, San Fernando, CA; Burbank Studios, Burbank, CA.

*Silliphant's listing as executive producer re-

180

sulted from his work on an early screenplay. According to Richard Kobritz, Silliphant wrote one of three scripts for a theatrical version. The script was not used, nor did Silliphant play an active role in producing SL; the credits reflect an "agreement with the studio because of his prior involvement with the project" (Kelley, "Salem's Lot" 18).

<u>The Shining</u>.

Warner Brothers/ Hawks Films, 1980. Produced in association with The Producer Circle Company: Robert Fryer, Martin Richards, Mary Lea Johnson. VHS, Beta: $69.95. 143 minutes. Rating: R.

Stanley Kubrick, producer/director.
Jan Harlan, executive producer.
Stanley Kubrick, director.
Brian Cook, assistant director.
Stanley Kubrick and Diane Johnson, screenplay.
John Alcott, director of photography.
Roy Walker, production design.
Ray Lovejoy, editor.
Tom Smith, make-up.
Milena Canonera, costumes
Wendy Carlos, music.
> Incorporating music by Bela Bartok, Krysztof Penderecki, Gyorgi Ligeti, Wendy Carlos and Rachel Elkin

<u>Cast</u>: Jack Nicholson . . . . Jack Torrance
Shelley Duvall . . . . Wendy Torrance
Danny Lloyd. . . . . Danny Torrance
Scatman Crothers . . . . . . Dick Hallorann
Barry Nelson . . . . Stuart Ullman
Philip Stone . . . . .Delbert Grady
Joe Turkel . . . . .Lloyd
Anne Jackson . . . . Doctor
Tony Burton. . . . . Larry Durkin
Lia Beldam . . . . . .Young woman in bathroom
Billie Gibson. . . . . .Old woman in bathroom
Barry Dennen . . . . Watson
David Baxt . . . . .Forest ranger 1
Manning Redwood. . . . . . . .Forest ranger 2
Lisa Burns . . . . Grady daughter 1
Louise Burns . . . . Grady daughter 2
Robin Pappas . . . . .Nurse
Alison Coleridge . . . . . Ullman´s secretary
Burnell Tucker . . . . .Policeman
Jana Sheldon . . . . Stewardess
Kate Phelps. . . . . . .Overlook Receptionist
Norman Gay . . . . .Injured guest

Location shots: Timberline Lodge, Mount Hood OR
Budget: $19,000,000.

Silver Bullet

Based on Cycle of the Werewolf. Paramount; North
Carolina Film Corporation (Dino de Laurentiis),
1985. VHS, Beta: $79.95. 95 minutes. Rating:
R.

Martha Schumacher, producer.
Dino de Laurentiis, executive producer.
John M. Eckert, associate producer.
Daniel Attias, director.
Stephen King, screenplay.
Armando Nannuzzi, director of photography.
Giorgio Postiglione, production designer.
Daniel Loewenthal, film editor.
Jay Chattaway, music.
Carlo Rambaldi, creator of creatures.

Cast: Gary Busey . . . . Uncle Red
      Everitt McGill . . . . .Reverend Lowe
      Corey Haim . . . . Marty Coslaw
      Megan Follows . . . . .Jane Coslaw
      Robin Groves . . . . Nan Coslaw
      Leon Russom . . . . Bob Coslaw
      Terry O'Quinn. . . . . . . Sheriff Joe Haller
      Bill Smitrovitch . . . . .Andy Furton
      Joe Wright . . . . .Brady Kinkaid
      Kent Broadhurst . . . . .Herb Kinkaid
      Heather Simmons . . . . . . Tammy Sturmfuller
      Rebecca Fleming . . . . . . .Mrs. Sturmfuller
      Lawrence Tierney. . . . . Owen Knopfler
      James A. Baffico. . . . . . .Milt Sturmfuller
      William Newman. . . . . Virgil Cuts
      Sam Stoneburner . . . . .Mayor O'Banion
      Lonnie Moore. . . . . Billy McLaren
      Rick Pasotto. . . . . .Aspinall
      Cassidy Eckert. . . . . .Girl
      Wendy Walker. . . . . Stella Randolph
      Michael Lague . . . . . . .Stella's boyfriend
      Myra Mailloux . . . . Stella's mother
      William Brown . . . . Bobby Robertson
      Herb Harton . . . . Elmo Zinneman
      David Hart. . . . . .Pete Sylvester
      Graham Smith. . . . . Porter Zinneman
      Paul Butler . . . . .Edgar Rounds
      Crysta Field. . . . . .Maggie Andrews
      Julius Leflore. . . . . .Smokey

```
Roxanne Aalan . . . . . . . .Uncle Red's girl
Pearl Jones . . . . . . . . . . Mrs. Thayer
Ish Jones, Jr.  . . . . . . . . .Mr. Thayer
Steven White. . . . . . . . . . .Outfielder
Conrad McLaren. . . . . . . . . . . . . Mac
Tovah Feldshuh. . . . .Voice of grown-up Jane
James Gammon. . . . . . . . . Arnie Westrum
```

Filmed on location in Wilmington, NC.

The Woman in the Room.

Darkwoods, 1983. Granite Entertainment. VHS, Beta: $79.95. 30 minutes.

Gregory Melton, producer.
Mark Vance, associate producer.
Douglas Venturelli, executive producer.
Michael Sloan, production manager.
Frank Darabont, director.
Frank Darabont, screenwriter.
Juan Ruiz Anchia, cinematographer.
Frank Darabont and Kevin Rock, editors.
Gregory Melton, art director.

Cast: Michael Cornelison . . . . .John
      Dee Croxton. . . . . Mother
      Brian Libby. . . . . Prisoner
      Bob Brunson. . . . . Guard #1
      George Russell . . . . Guard #2

Released as one segment of "Two Mini-Features from
. . . Stephen King´s Night Shift Collection."

The Word Processor of the Gods

Laurel Entertainment, Inc.; Tales from the Darkside series. 19 November 1985.

William Teitler, producer.
Richard P. Rubenstein, George A. Romero, and Jerry Golod; executive producers.
David E. Vogel, executive in charge of production.
Michael Gornick, director.
Michael McDowell, teleplay.

Cast: Bruce Davidson . . . . . . .Richard Hagstrom
Karen Shallo . . . . .Lina Hagstrom
Bill Cain. . . . . Mr. Nordhoff
Jon Matthews . . . . Jonathan
Patrick Piccininni . . . . Seth

Films in Production

Overdrive (Also referred to as <u>Maximum Overdrive</u>). Based on "Trucks" (<u>NS</u>). North Carolina Film Corporation (Dino de Laurentiis). Release date: July 18, 1986.

Martha Schumacher, producer.
Stephen King, director.
Stephen King, screenwriter.
Giorgio Postigilione, production design.
Steve Gallich, special effects.
Julius LeFoore, stunts.
Armando Nannuzzi, cinematographer.
<u>Cast</u>: Emilio Estevez . . . . . . .Bill Robertson
     Pat Hingle . . . . Hendershot
     Laura Harrington . . . . Brett
Budget: $10,000,000.

The Body. Based on "The Body" (<u>DS</u>). Release date: July 18, 1986.
Rob Reiner, director.

The Running Man. Taft Entertainment. Scheduled to begin filming in October, 1985, in Edmonton, Alberta, Canada; re-located to Los Angeles, 1986. George Cosmatos, director (<u>Rambo</u>)
<u>Cast</u>: Christopher Reeve; re-cast with Arnold Schwarzenegger.

Pet Sematary. Screenplay by Stephen King. With George A. Romero. Filming site: Maine. Scheduled to begin production, March 1986.
Richard Rubenstein, producer.
George A. Romero, director.

The Stand. Screenplay by Stephen King. With George A. Romero. An early draft called for a two-part film: <u>The Stand, I</u> would deal with the flu epidemic; <u>The Stand, II</u>, with the struggle against the Dark Man. The third draft incorporates both into a three-hour film. Filming site: Texas.

Training Exercise. From a treatment by Stephen King. Produced through North Carolina Film Corporation (Dino de Laurentiis). Estimated schedule: 1987.

187

IT. ABC-TV mini-series. Projected date: Fall, 1987.

The Talisman. Option discussed by Steven Spielberg.

The Long Walk.

King´s screenplays (not produced)

Battleground
Children of the Corn
Cujo
The Dead Zone
Night Shift
The Shotgunners
The Shining
Something Wicked This Way Comes (Bradbury)

King has been involved in a number of other film possibilities:

> Creepshow II, a sequel to Creepshow. The project is critical if not dead.

> Martin Poll Productions optioned "Battleground," "Strawberry Spring," and "I Know What You Need" for an NBC-TV anthology. The project died.

> Milton Subotsky optioned "The Lawnmower Man," "Trucks," and "The Mangler" for an anthology film, plus rights to "The Ledge," "Quitters, Inc.," and "Sometimes They Come Back." King arranged with Subotsky for rights to produce Cat´s Eye.

King has said that every story in NS except "Jerusalem´s Lot" has been discussed as a film.

WORKS CITED AND CONSULTED

Alberton, Jim, and Peter S. Perakos. "The Shining." Cinefantastique (Fall 1978): 74.

Alexander, Alex E. "Stephen King's Carrie: A Universal Fairy Tale." Journal of Popular Film and Television, 13 (1979): 282-288.

Bentkowski, Kent Daniel. "King's 'Gramma' Makes Her Small Screen Debut." Castle Rock (April 1985): 5, 8.

Blue, Tyson. "King Goes in Overdrive." Twilight Zone Magazine (February 1986): 30-31.

---------- "SK Interviewed on Overdrive Movie Set." Castle Rock (November 1985): 1, 4-6.

Brown, Garrett. "The Steadicam and 'The Shining.'" American Cinematographer (August 1980): 786.

Casey, Susan. "On the Set of 'Salem's Lot." Fangoria, 4 (February 1980): 38-42.

Cavett, Dick, moderator. Horror Panel I, II: Transcription of The Dick Cavett Show, 30/31 October 1980. New York: Journal Graphics. Other guests included Ira Levin, Peter Straub, and George A. Romero.

Chatman, Seymour. "What Novels Can Do That Films Can't (and Vice Versa)." In "On Narrative. Ed. W. J. T. Mitchell. Chicago IL: University of Chicago Press, 1981. Rpt. of Critical Inquiry, 7, No. 1 (August 1980); 7, No. 4 (Summer 1981).

Christensen, Dan. "Stephen King: Living in 'Constant, Deadly Terror.'" Bloody Best of Fangoria (February 1982): 30-33.

Chute, David. "King of the Night: An Interview with Stephen King." Take One (January 1979): 33-38.

Cohen, D. Lawrence. Carrie (screenplay). Culver City CA: Red Bank Films, Inc., January 1976.

Collings, Michael R. The Many Facets of Stephen King. Mercer Island WA: Starmont House, 1985.

---------- Stephen King as Richard Bachman. Mercer Island WA: Starmont House, 1985.

---------- and David A. Engebretson. The Shorter Works of Stephen King. Mercer Island WA: Starmont House, 1985.

189

Crist, Judith. "This Week's Movies." <u>TV Guide</u> 30
    April-6 May 1983: A5-A6.
Darabont, Frank. Letter to Michael R. Collings.
    23 August 1985.
Dimeo, Steve. "Stephen King Script Little More
    Than Sheep in Wolf's Clothes." <u>Cinefantas-</u>
    <u>tique</u> (March 1986: 43, 54.
Edel, Leon. "Novel and Camera. In <u>The Theory of</u>
    <u>the Novel: New Essays</u>. Ed. John Halperin.
    New York: Oxford University Press, 1974:
    177-187.
Ehlers, Leigh H. "<u>Carrie</u>: Book and Film." In <u>Ideas</u>
    <u>of Order: Literature and Film</u>. Ed. Peter Rup-
    pert and others. Tallahassee FL: University
    Presses of Florida, 1980: 39-50. Rpt. in <u>Lit-</u>
    <u>erature and Film Quarterly</u> (Spring 1981):
    32-39.
Ellison, Harlan. "Part Two: In Which We Discover
    Why the Children Don't Look Like Their Par-
    ents." <u>Castle Rock</u> (March 1986): 1, 4-6.
    Rpt. from <u>The Magazine of Fantasy and Science</u>
    <u>Fiction</u>.
Everitt, David. "Stephen King's Children of the
    Corn." <u>Fangoria</u> 35 (1985): 42-45.
---------- "Stephen King's Silver Bullet." <u>Fangor-</u>
    <u>ia</u> 48 (1985): 30-32.
Fiedler, Leslie A. "The Death and Re-birth of the
    Novel." In <u>The Theory of the Novel: New</u>
    <u>Essays</u>. Ed. John Halperin. New York: Oxford
    University Press, 1974, 189-209.
Foster, Alan Dean. <u>The Thing</u>. New York: Bantam,
    [n.d., Science Fiction Book Club edition].
    Rpt. of 1981 MCA edition.
French, Lawrence. "Cat's Eye." <u>Cinefantastique</u>
    (October 1985): 36.
Gagne, Paul. "Creepshow." <u>Cinefantastique</u> (Septem-
    ber/October 1982): 17-35.
---------- "Stephen King." <u>Cinefantastique</u> (Decem-
    ber/January 1983/84): 4-5.
Garcia, Guy D. "People." <u>Time</u> 9 September 1985:
    63.
Gifford, Thomas. "Stephen King's Quartet." <u>Wash-</u>
    <u>ington Post Book World</u> 22 August 1982.
Glut, Donald F. <u>The Dracula Book</u>. Metuchen NJ:
    Scarecrow Press, 1975.
Goldberg, Lee. "Now Re-Entering 'The Twilight
    Zone.'" <u>Starlog</u> (October 1985): 38-40.
Grant, Charles M. "A King-Size Interview." <u>Mon-</u>

sterland (June 1985): 27-30.

Gray, Paul. "Master of Postliterate Prose." Time 30 August 1982: 87.

Handling, Piers, ed. The Shape of Rage: The Films of David Cronenberg. Toronto, Canada: General Publishing Ltd., 1983.

Harper, L. Christine. "Reel Futures." Mile High Futures 22 January 1984.

Herndon, Ben. "New Adventures in the Scream Trade." Twilight Zone Magazine (December 1985): 6A-7A.

---------- "Real Tube Terror." Twilight Zone Magazine (December 1985): 10A-10B.

---------- "The Twilight Zone." Cinefantastique (March 1986): 22-23, 58.

Hewitt, Tim. "Overdrive." Cinefantastique (March 1986): 9.

Hofsess, Jim. "The Shining Example of Kubrick." Los Angeles Times, Calendar section, 1 June 1980: 1.

Hogan, David J. "Carpenter Borrowed King's Car, But Doesn't Know How to Drive." Cinefantastique (May 1984): 56-57.

---------- "Firestarter [I]." Cinefantastique (May 1984): 28-30.

---------- "Firestarter [II]." Cinefantastique (September 1984): 16-25.

Hurwood, Bernhardt J. Vampires. New York: Quick Fox, 1981.

Jameson, Richard T. "Kubrick's Shining." Film Comment (July-August 1980): 28-32.

Johnson, Kim. "Christine: Stephen King and John Carpenter Take a Joy Ride to Terror." Mediascene (1984).

Kael, Pauline. "Devolution." The New Yorker 1 June 1980: 130-147.

Kawin, Bruce. Review of The Fury. Take One, 6 (May 1978): 7.

Keeler, Greg. "The Shining: Ted Kramer Has a Nightmare." Journal of Popular Film and Television (Winter 1981): 2-8.

Kelley, Bill. "Effects Man Roy Arbogast Was in Charge of the Film's Amazing Automotive Star." Cinefantastique (May 1984): 56-57.

---------- "Salem's Lot: Filming Horror for Television." Cinefantastique (Winter 1979): 8-21.

Kennedy, Harlan. "Kubrick Goes Gothic." American Film (June 1980): 49-52.

King, Stephen. <u>Cujo</u>. New York: Viking, 1981.
---------- <u>Danse Macabre</u>. New York: Everest House, 1981.
---------- "Digging the Boogens." <u>Twilight Zone</u> (July 1982): 9-10.
---------- "The Evil Dead: Why You Haven´t Seen It Yet . . . and Why You Ought To." <u>Twilight Zone</u> (November 1982): 20-22.
---------- "Horrors." <u>TV Guide</u> 30 October 1982: 54-58.
---------- "The Horrors of ´79." <u>Rolling Stone</u> 27 December 1979-10 January 1980.
---------- "How to Scare a Woman to Death." <u>Murderess, Ink: The Better Half of the Mystery</u>. Ed. Dilys Winn. New York: Workman, 1980: 173-175.
---------- "Lists That Matter (Number 8)." <u>Castle Rock</u> (September 1985):7.
---------- "Market Writer and the Ten Bears." <u>Writer´s Digest</u> (November 1973) 10-13. Rpt. in <u>Kingdom of Fear</u>. Ed. Tim Underwood and Chuck Miller. Columbia PA: Underwood-Miller, 1986.
---------- "Notes on Horror." <u>Quest</u> (June 1981): 28-31, 87. Reprint from <u>Danse Macabre</u>.
---------- "On <u>The Shining</u> and Other Perpetrations." <u>Whispers</u> 17/18 (August 1982): 11-16.
---------- "Pet Sematary." First-draft screenplay, 1985.
---------- <u>Silver Bullet</u>. New York: NAL/Signet, 1985.
---------- "Special Make-Up Effects and the Writer." In <u>Grande Illusions</u>. By Tom Savini. Pittsburgh PA: Imagine, Inc., 1983: 6-7.
---------- "Stephen King: His Creepiest Movies." <u>USA Today</u> 27 August 1985.
---------- "Trucks." First-draft screenplay. 8 February 1985.
---------- "Why We Crave Horror Movies." <u>Playboy</u> (January 1981): 150-154, 237-246.
Kroll, Jack. "Stanley Kubrick´s Horror Show." <u>Newsweek</u> 26 May 1980: 96-99.
Leerhsen, Charles. "The Titans of Terror." <u>Newsweek</u> 24 December 1984: 61-62.
Leibowitz, Flo, and Lynn Jeffress. "The Shining." <u>Film Quarterly</u> (Spring 1981): 45-51.
Lichtenstein, Allen. "Science Fiction Book Versus Movie Audiences: Implications for the Teach-

ing of Science Fiction." Extrapolation, 24,
No. 1 (1983): 47-56.
Lightman, Herb. "Photographing Stanley Kubrick´s
The Shining: An Interview with John Alcott."
American Cinematographer (August 1980): 760.
Lorenz, Janet E. "Carrie." In Magill´s Survey of
Cinema. 2nd series. Vol. II. Englewood Cliffs
NJ: Salem Press, 1981:408-411.
Lucas, Tim. "David Cronenberg´s Dead Zone."
Cinefantastique (December/January 1983/1984):
24-31.
---------- and contributing editors of Video
Times. Your Movie Guide to Horror Video Tapes
and Discs. Publications International, 1985.
---------- Your Movie Guide to Science Fic-
tion/Fantasy Video Tapes and Discs. Publica-
tions International, 1985.
Macklin, F. Anthony. "Understanding Kubrick: The
Shining." Journal of Popular Film and Televi-
sion (Summer 1982): 93-95.
Martin, R. H. [Bob]. "A Casual Chat with Mr.
George A. Romero." Fangoria (October 1982).
---------- "Christine." Fangoria 32 (1984): 14-17.
---------- "George Romero on Day of the Dead and
Pet Sematary. Fangoria 48 (1985): 43-47.
---------- "Keith Gordon and Christine." Fangoria
32 (1984):19-22.
---------- "Mark Lester Directs Firestarter." Fan-
goria 36 (1984): 12-15.
---------- "On the Set of Firestarter." Fangoria
35 (1984):56-59.
---------- "On (and Off) the Set of Creepshow: Tom
Savini at Work; Stephen King at Home." Fan-
goria (May 1982): 40-43.
---------- "Stephen King on Overdrive and Pet Sem-
atary." Fangoria 48 (1985): 10-12, 64.
Mayersberg, Paul. "The Overlook Hotel." Sight and
Sound (Winter 1980/81): 54-57.
Modderno, Craig. "I´d Really Like to Write a Rock
´n´ Roll Novel." USA Today 10 May 1985.
Monash, Paul, and Larry Cohen. Carrie (screenplay;
first draft).
Naha, Ed. "Frontrow Seats at the ´Creepshow.´"
Fangoria (May 1982): 46-50.
Nelson, Thomas Allen. Kubrick: Inside a Film Ar-
tist´s Maze. Bloomington: Indiana University
Press, 1982.
Novak, Ralph. "Firestarter." People 28 May 1984:

193

12.

Neuhaus, Cable. "Firestarter's Premier." People 28
May 1984: 64.

Perakos, Peter. "Interview with Stephen King."
Cinefantastique (Winter 1978): 12-15.

---------- "Stephen King on Carrie, The Shining,
Etc." Cinefantastique, 8 (1978): 12-15.

Rhetts, JoAnn. "The Titan of Terror." Escondido
Times-Advocate 3 October 1985: 30-31.

Rockett, W. H. "The Door Ajar: Structure and Con-
vention in Horror Films That Would Terrify."
Journal of Popular Film and Television, 10,
No. 3 (Fall 1981): 130-136.

Salamon, Julie. "Horrormonger Stephen King on
Screen." Wall Street Journal 25 April 1985:
34.

Sallee, Wayne Allen. "It's Really Only a Game."
Castle Rock (April 1986): 2.

Scapperotti, Dan. "Gary Zeller." Cinefantastique
(September 1984): 22. Special effects for
Firestarter.

Schickel, Richard. "Red Herrings and Refusals."
Time 2 June 1980: 69.

Schow, David. "Return of the Curse of the Son of
Mr. King: Book Two." Whispers, 17/18 (August
1982): 49-56.

"Stephen King's The Woman in the Room." Variety 19
September 1985. Advertisement for PBS.

Straub, Peter. "Meeting Stevie." In Fear Itself:
The Horror Fiction of Stephen King. Eds. Tim
Underwood and Chuck Miller. New York: New
American Library/Plume, 1984. Rpt. of 1982
Underwood-Miller edition.

Sragow, Michael. "Stephen King's Creepshow: The
Aesthetics of Gross-out." Rolling Stone 25
November 1982: 48, 54.

Telotte, J. P. "The Horror Mythos and Val Lewton's
Isle of the Dead." Journal of Popular Film
and Television, 10, No. 3 (Fall 1981):
119-129.

Titterington, P. L. "Kubrick and The Shining."
Sight and Sound (Spring 1981): 117-121.

Verniere, James. "Screen Previews: Dead Zone."
Twilight Zone (November/December 1983): 52-
55.

Wiater, Stanley. "Collaboration in Terror."
Bloody Best of Fangoria (1982):28-29.

---------- and Roger Anker. "Horror Partners."

<u>Fangoria</u> 42 (1986): 10-13.

Williams, Sharon. "Stephen King's 'Cycle of the Werewolf' Becomes <u>Silver Bullet</u>." <u>Fantasy Films</u> (October 1985): 20-22.

Wilson, Gahan. "TZ Screen." <u>Twilight Zone Magazine</u> (October 1985): 96-98.

Winter, Douglas E. "Stephen King's Art of Darkness." <u>Fantasy Review</u> (November 1984): 8-15.

Wood, Robin. "Return of the Repressed." <u>Film Comment</u> (July-August 1978): 25-32.

Yarbro, Chelsea Quinn. "Cinderella's Revenge: Twists on Fairy Tale and Mythic Themes in the Work of Stephen King." In <u>Fear Itself: The Horror Fiction of Stephen King</u>. Eds. Tim Underwood and Chuck Miller. New York: New American Library/Plume, 1984: 63-74. Rpt. of 1982 Underwood-Miller edition.

Zoglin, Richard. "Giving Hollywood the Chills: Stephen King's Scary Bestsellers Become Hot Film Properties." <u>Time</u> 9 January 1984.

SELECTIVE INDEX OF NAMES AND TITLES

This index excludes references from the "Filmography" or "Works Cited and Consulted"; it also excludes many references to Stephen King, since his name appears frequently in the text.

113; "The Mangler"
161; Misery 27; "The
Mist" 2; "The Monkey"
2; "Mrs. Todd's
Shortcut" 14; Night
Shift 1, 114, 117,
131, 158; "The Raft"
2, 117, 142; "The
Reach" 2, 147; "The
Revelations of 'Becka
Paulson" 161; Skele-
ton Crew 1, 27, 117,
147, 161; "Slade"
133; "Trucks" 157-162
Kirby, Terry: 114
Kobritz, Richard: 42-52
(see also Salem's
Lot)
Konchalavsky, Andrei:
91
Kramer vs. Kramer: 61
Kubrick, Stanley: 1, 2,
13, 16, 21, 53-64,
66, 70, 82, 94, 95;
Barry Lindon 58-59; A
Clockwork Orange 57,
58, 60; Day of the
Flight 57; Dr.
Strangelove 58, 60;
Flying Padre 57; Fear
and Desire 57; Kil-
ler's Kiss 57; The
Killing 57-58; Lolita
58; Paths of Glory
57-58; The Seafarer
57; Spartacus 57-58;
2001 55, 57, 58, 60,
62, 64, 143 (see also
The Shining)
Lancaster, Bill: 4, 123
Lancaster, Burt: 126
Langella, Frank: 15
Lauter, Ed: 88
Lee, Kaiulani: 88
Leerhsen, Charles: 11
Lester, Mark: 121-128;
Class of 1984 123;
Gold of the Amazon

Women 123; Roller
Boogie 123; Steel
Arena 124; Tricia's
Wedding 124; Truck
Stop Women 124;
Twilight of the
Mayans 124 (see also
Firestarter)
Let's Scare Jessica to
Death: 26
Lewton, Val: 19-20
Libby, Brian: 150
Lichtenstein, Alan: 15
Ligeti, Gyorgy: 58, 59
Long Walk, The: 188
Lord of the Flies
(Golding): 13
Lord of the Rings: 10
Lovecraft, H. P.: 21,
71, 154-155; The
Colour Out of Space
71; Necronomicon 154
Lucas, Tim: 94, 127
Lugosi, Bela: 15, 45,
46, 113
McDowell, Michael: 148
McGill, Everitt: 140
McMillan, Kenneth: 130,
131
Macklin, Anthony F.:
59-61
Marshall, E.G.: 65, 78
Martin, R. H. (Bob):
67, 121, 124
Mann, Stanley: 123
Masefield, Joe: 114
Mason, James: 46, 52
Maze, The (film): 56
Miller, Arthur: 53
Missing in Action: 113
Monash, Paul: 42-44
Monroe, Marilyn: 131
Morgan, Donald M.: 107
Munster,, Bill: 28
Murnau, F. W.: 15,
45-47, 52
Nalder, Reggie: 46, 52
Nelson, Thomas Allen:

199

www.ingramcontent.com/pod-product-compliance
Lightning Source LLC
Chambersburg PA
CBHW030521100426
42813CB00001B/110